ORIGINS OF THE
LOST POETIC ARCHIVES
FROM AN UNKNOWN SCHOLAR

SPECIAL EDITION

B-POET

PROMINENT
BOOKS

5830 E 2nd St, Ste 7000 #9983
Casper, Wyoming, 82609
USA

CONTENTS

Special Edition
(Bonus Material)

Special Edition
(Bonus Poems)

SPECIAL EDITION

ORIGINS OF THE
LOST POETIC ARCHIVES

FROM AN UNKNOWN SCHOLAR

B-POET

Experience B-poet's entire discovery of the *Lost Poetic Archives at…*
Originsofthelostpoeticarchives.godaddysites.com

A MESSAGE DESTINED FOR TRUTH

(Dimeter Version)

Belonging in
A social class
Of your own can
Inspire all
Who dare to live
Out loud views from
Their personal
Aspirations

Beyond self-said
Adversity
An inner voice
Of reasoning
Within themselves
Now opens up
Possible doors

To explore by
Availing souls
For a passage
Signified as
A clear *Message*
Destined For Truth
Used to ignite

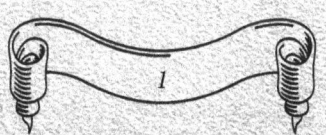

A personal
Transformation
Meant to embrace
The future breed
Of tomorrow
We all know as
Humanity

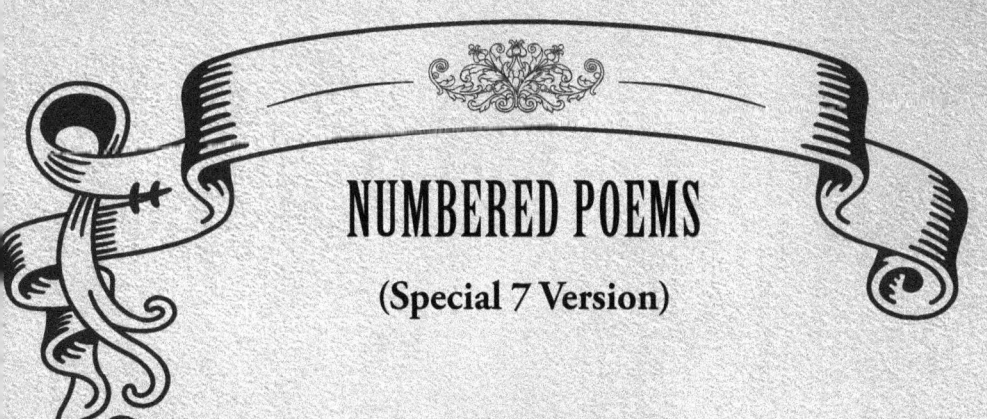

NUMBERED POEMS

(Special 7 Version)

Charted poetic journeys
Signify symbolic themes
Numerically over
430 themes
May surface as **Numbered Poems**
Near countless hieroglyphic

Tales found at the end of
This literary groundwork
Were *Edified* and *Composed*
Like solid calligraphy
Word bricks fitted within a
Written Wall Of Destiny*

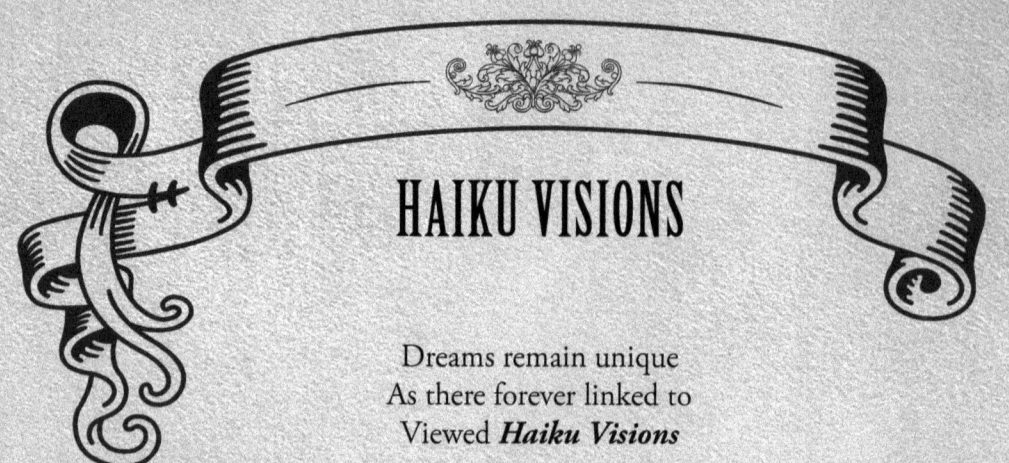

HAIKU VISIONS

Dreams remain unique
As there forever linked to
Viewed *Haiku Visions*

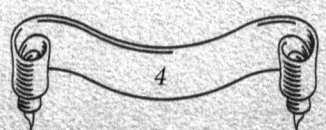

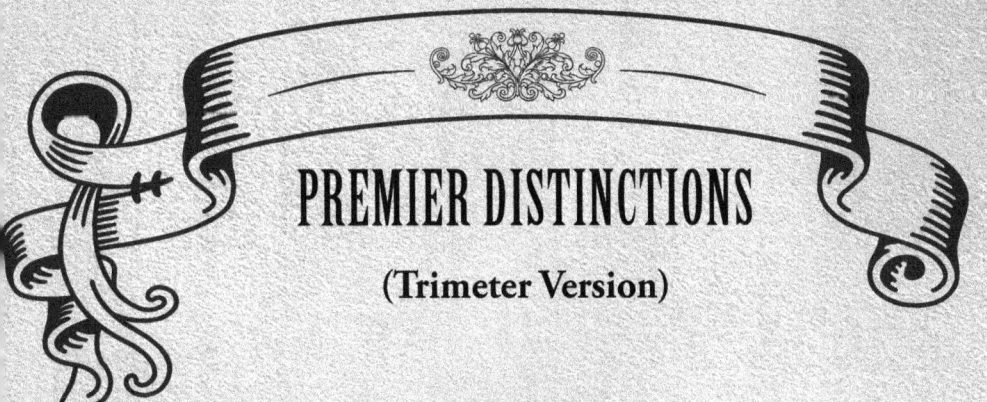

PREMIER DISTINCTIONS

(Trimeter Version)

Literary building
Blocks were left to remain
In a scholar's penned vault
Once his masterpiece was
Completed it remained

Hidden in compartments
Of a secret diction
Chest where these vested words
Gave life to a scholar's
Shiny armor's tin fold

Clever and *Prophetic*...
Eloquent and *Bold Verse*...

Dictated the course of
A known visionary
Character's existing
Collaborator's twist
Of scene rhyme forged a timed

Sublime symbolic dream
During a groundbreaking
Endorsed ceremony
Of an unknown scholar's
Post ***Premier Distinctions***

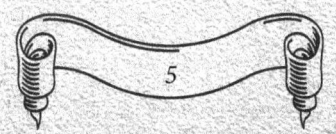

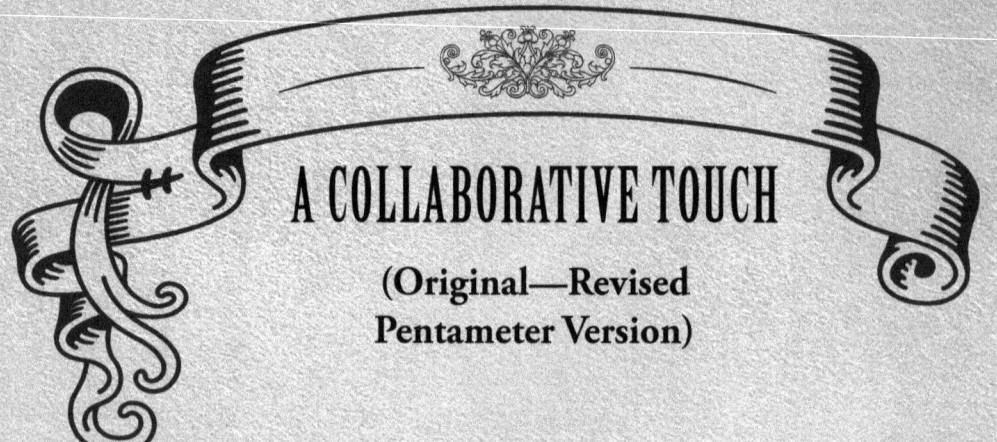

A COLLABORATIVE TOUCH

(Original—Revised
Pentameter Version)

Brushstrokes of alphabetic wizardry
Share a dual legacy as two like minds
Chose to shed light on worded symphonies

Where rare distinctive styles embodied voiced
Written chemistry decoratively
Penned working miracles reminiscent

Of _**Cleverly Written Montage**_* once left
Behind enough relevant clues to view
_A_ rarefied **Collaborative Touch**

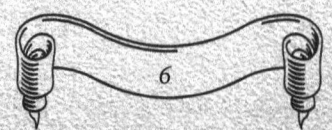

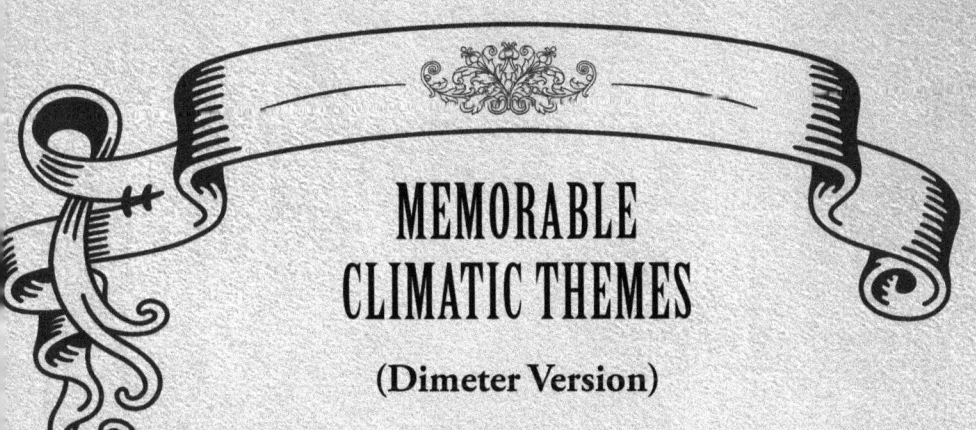

MEMORABLE
CLIMATIC THEMES

(Dimeter Version)

__Cherished Breaths__* from
__Two Loving Doves__*
Resonated
A kindred love
Existed well

Beyond brethren's
Said beliefs as
Humanities
Likeliness had
Helped to shape an

Absolute cloud's
Significance
Acted out vows
Transiently
Above our heads

Aiding to change
Our forecasted
Jet streams into
Memorable
Climatic Themes

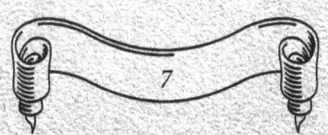

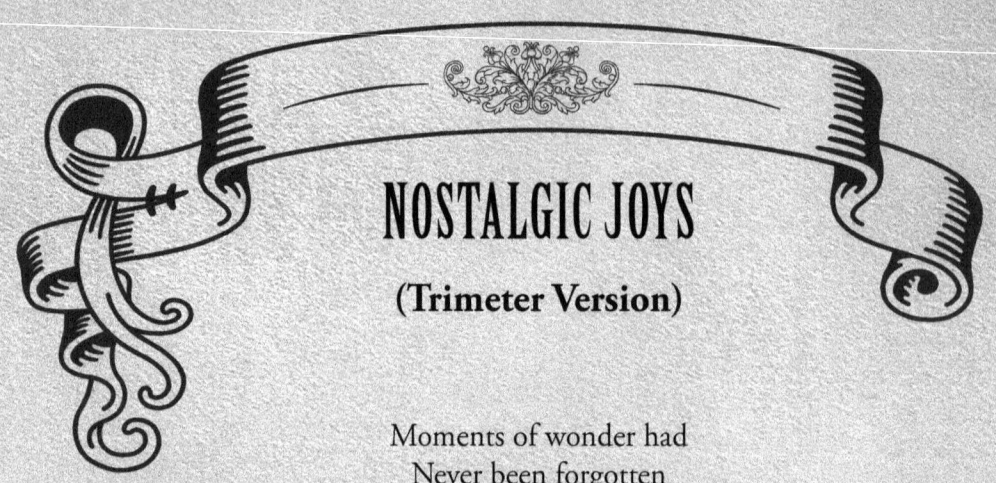

NOSTALGIC JOYS

(Trimeter Version)

Moments of wonder had
Never been forgotten
Since time possesses our
Best memories brought to

Life the question for why
Personal precious viewed
Moments reserved this calm
Heartfelt assurance now

Depicting forever
Blue skies in a pleasant
Utopia so each
Being could befriend their

Nostalgic Joys as known
Coping armor against
The world's future sorrows
Near tomorrow's banquet

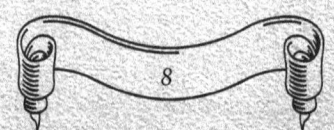

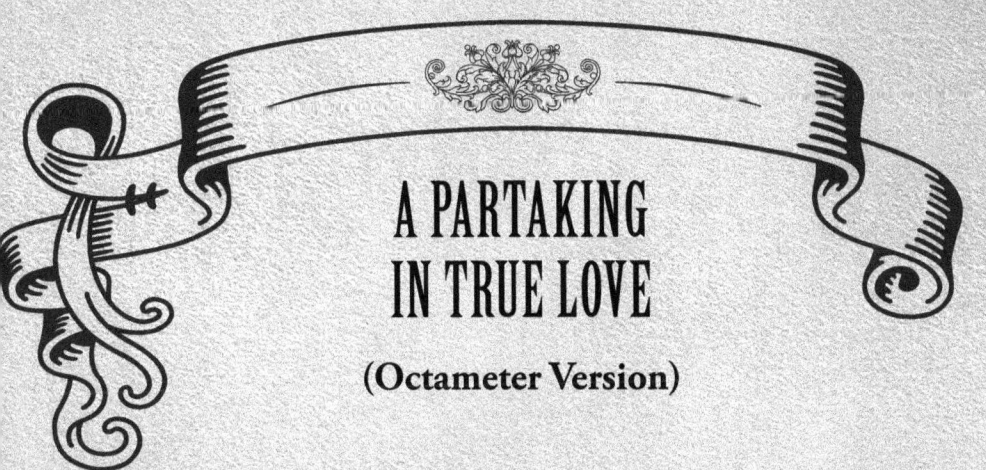

A PARTAKING
IN TRUE LOVE

(Octameter Version)

The core of sincerity's
Heartfelt devotions
From an unknown

Scholar shines
An unparalleled depth
From a loving wishing well

Rich with passion
Existing only
To quench desired

Actions
Of veering needs
Soulful mates may vow

To indulge in
Escapades
Worth more than

Wealth's estimated
Veiled price
Forever tips the scales

Within the heartfelt eyes
Of commitment's allurement
Penned alibis

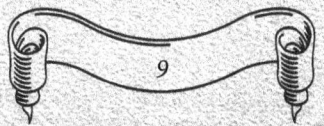

Are brought to life
On a written stage
Seen from above

Mezzanines of *A* valiant heart's
Estranged
Partaking In True Love

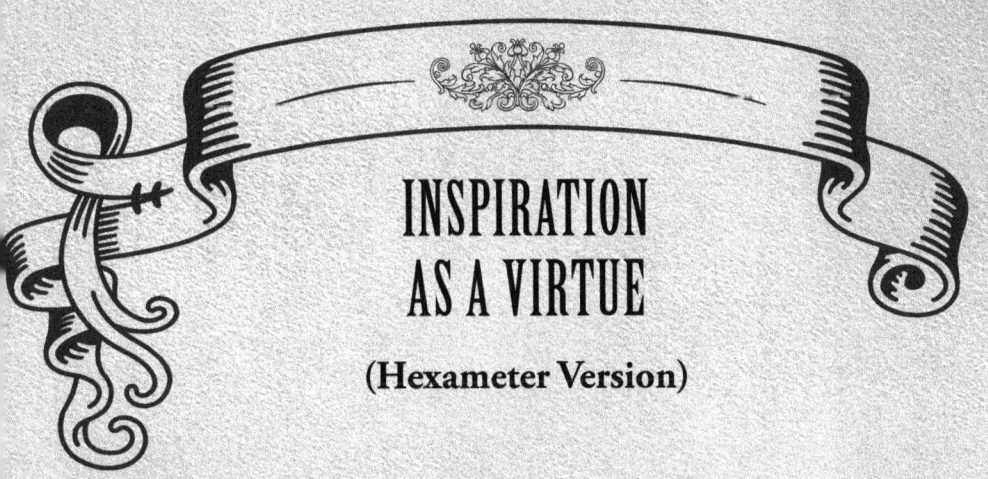

INSPIRATION AS A VIRTUE

(Hexameter Version)

It's engraved in the morality of conscious
Penmanship if embraced its known crafty gesture to
Preserve spirits in times of *doubt* and *crisis* drawn
Out of an alternate view where new world perspectives
Encouragingly contribute to sound clues in
A darkened sky's enlightenment fortune since
Chanced ***Inspiration As A Virtue*** veils self-spirited innocence

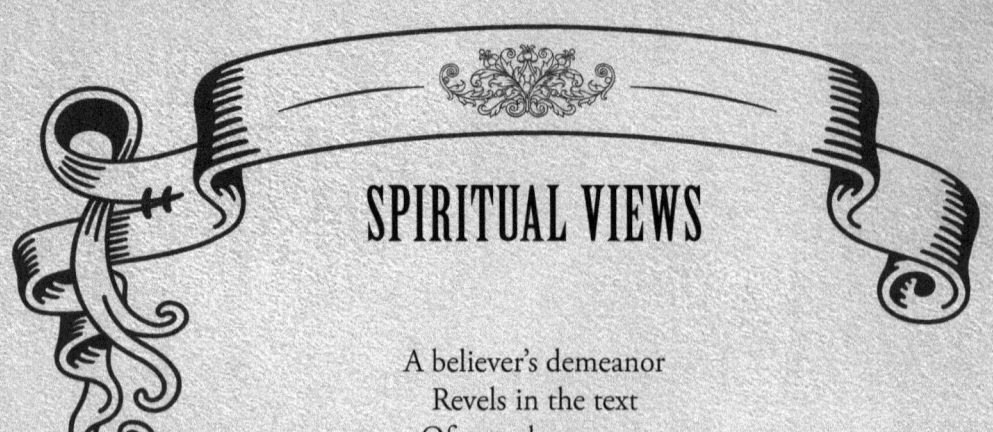

SPIRITUAL VIEWS

A believer's demeanor
Revels in the text
Of sacred messages
Written from divinity's ink
Sets the stage
For a grand revival scene
Pews of admiration

Were filled
With convened admirers
Carrying golden scrolls
Of their own
Who're willing to watch
Actualized rituals unfold
From chosen esteemed altars

A hieroglyphic redeemer
Will only appeal to virtuous
Spiritual Views
Inside wholehearted
Lead individuals
Who've chosen to heal
A diverse forsaken venue

MEANINGFUL PEAKS
& VALLEYS

Vast terrains
Filled with
Peaks of inspiration
Offer the *highs* and *lows*
From rising expectations
Others supposedly
Love to

Anoint and *Keep*
Their viewpoints
As challenges for everyone else's
Self-led transformation
Prior to merited journeys
Through endless
Meaningful Peaks & Valleys

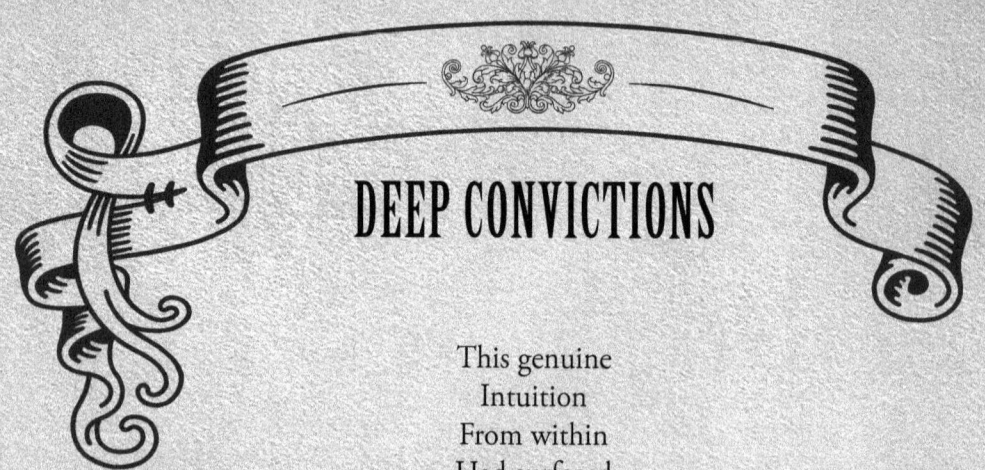

DEEP CONVICTIONS

This genuine
Intuition
From within
Had surfaced
Tension

Relevantly
Begun and
Brought forth
What matters
Internally

May shatter most
Externally
All of proven adversity's
Obstacles birthed
Faced images

Were now displayed
As broken fragments
Pieced from a
Vain gallery of discovered
Deep Convictions

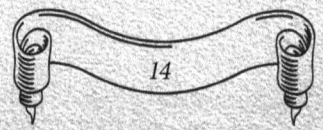

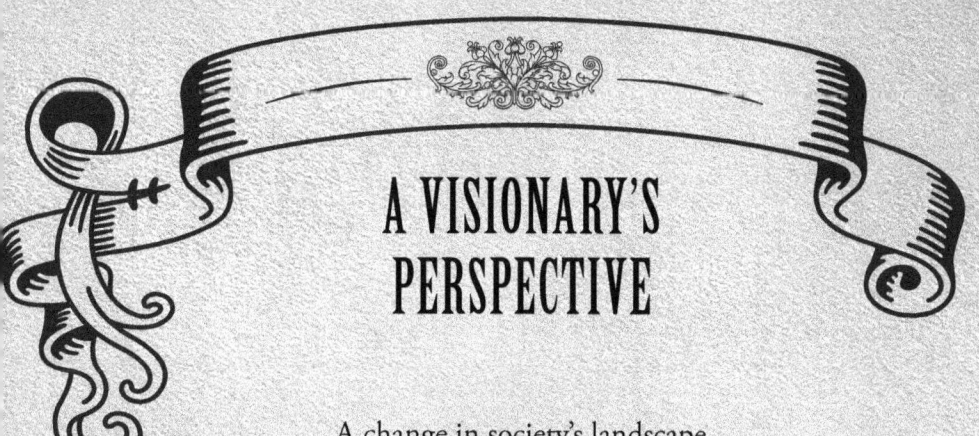

A VISIONARY'S PERSPECTIVE

A change in society's landscape
Where words
Are meant to encourage
Rather than tear down
Socially gifted reputations
On behalf of hypocrisy

Ill-advised truths
Have tarnished people's views
Who're on the verge
Of befriending
Destructive issues
Weighs out heavily as

A curfew belonging to indoctrinated
Views will inevitably fall into place
Beset by history at the hands
Of a familiar objective branded as
Revelational plateaus revealed
A Visionary's Perspective

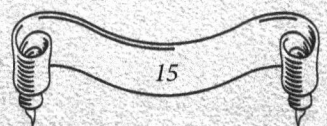

WISHFUL
THEORIES

(Octameter Version)

Why not have more mutual agreements among all different walks
Of life where finally there's a fine line of compromise behind
The faces seen sheltering belated minds of indifference bask on

Instinctually lead purposes have separated us as common
Courtesy renounced its position concerning
Our humane culture's need
To be revived by *Wishful Theories* sought out by
Pioneering thoughtful deeds of influence

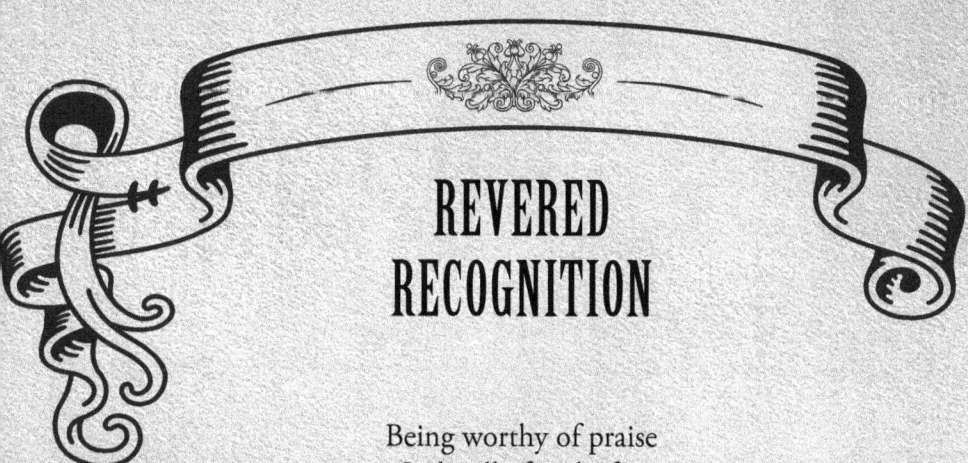

REVERED
RECOGNITION

Being worthy of praise
So hardly fought for
Molds a rare key
Presenting transcended opportunities
Used to open doors
For newcomers
Now on the scene

Who've appreciated
Your acquisition
Of a dawning pastime
Innovating it by
Casting them
As promising leads
In a longevity feature film

Starring…
Gratitude as
"A Chosen Genre's Reigned Era Of Inspiration"
Can now stand alone
As a deity prophetically
Proven to be bonded
With *Revered Recognition*

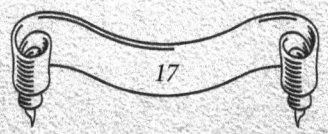

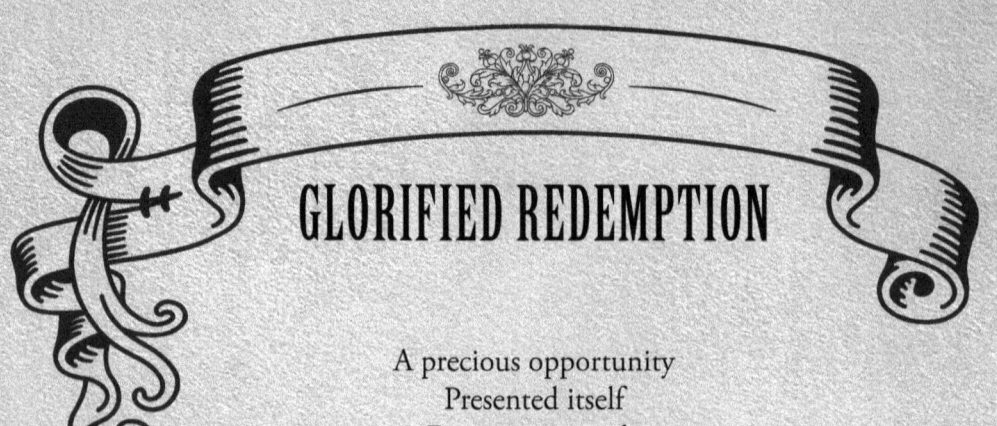

GLORIFIED REDEMPTION

A precious opportunity
Presented itself
For one time only
In the past tense
A forgotten time line
Of written miracles

Appeared as
A steady enlightened
Conversing compliance
With willful scholars
Who decided yes to join in
On rare heights of *Glorified Redemption*

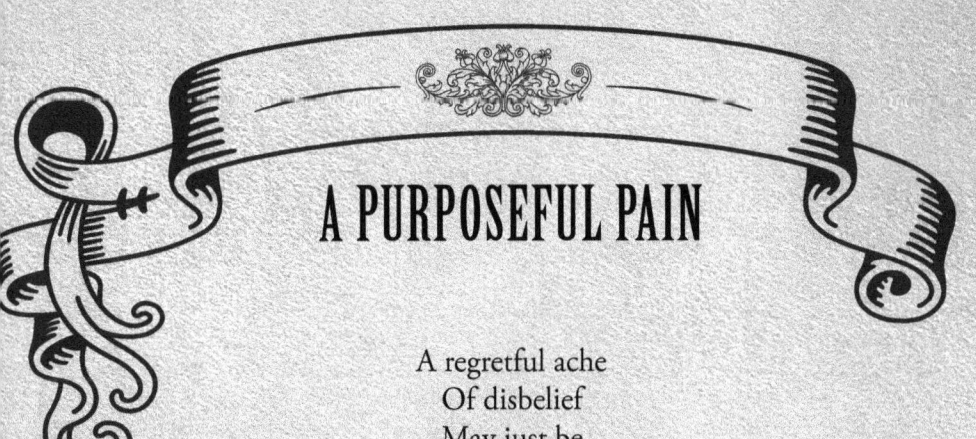

A PURPOSEFUL PAIN

A regretful ache
Of disbelief
May just be
An intended case
Called karma's spree
Beyond the heights
Of our conscious beliefs

A questioned aura within ourselves exemplifies
Who will govern?
What's left to gain?
Once we've experienced
Morality's needed
Lesson toward
A Purposeful Pain

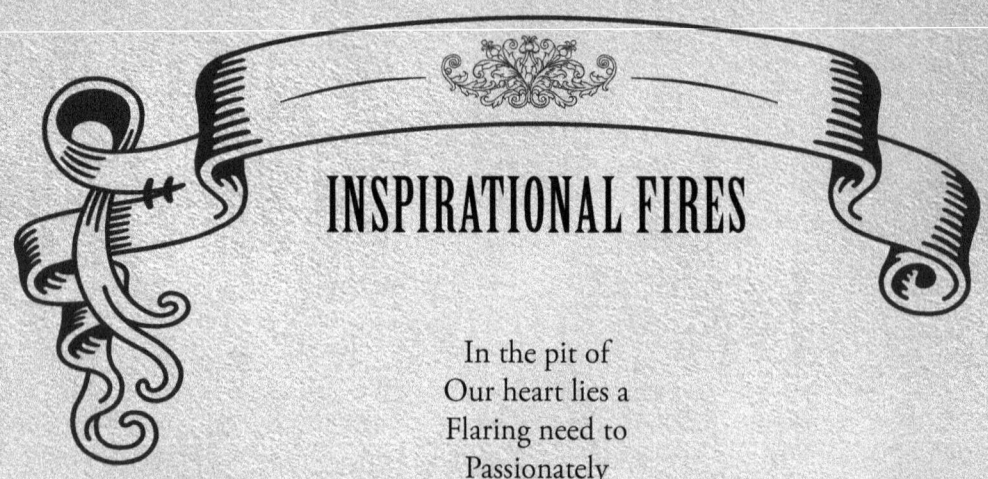

INSPIRATIONAL FIRES

In the pit of
Our heart lies a
Flaring need to
Passionately
Perceive
Favorable

Desired destinies
As a haven
Reality's
Grip on
Everyone's physical sense
Will ultimately transpire

In the form
Of a canvassed future
That's only recognizable
As our own
Inspirational Fires
Glaring and *Blazing* from within our souls

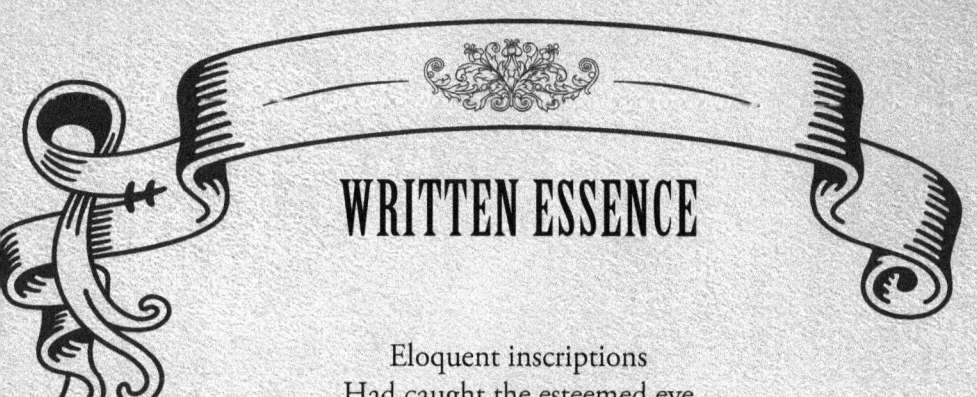

WRITTEN ESSENCE

Eloquent inscriptions
Had caught the esteemed eye
Belonging to a high level
Hieroglyphics art sculptor's caliber
Cultivated a based reality's

Societal culture
On the account of an *unknown scholar's*
Written Essence
Involving penned faith
Toward a new future's pastime

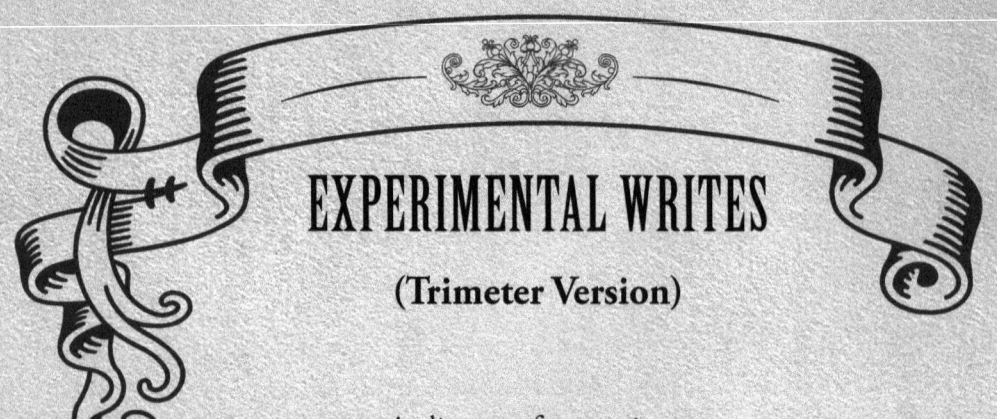

EXPERIMENTAL WRITES

(Trimeter Version)

A glimpse of rare written
Expression differed now
From any *style* or *deemed*
Genre made far from the
Norm of a clever heir's

Vocal viewpoint dares to
Be seen like widespread thoughts
Floating effortlessly
Within the sky's cloud of
Experimental Writes

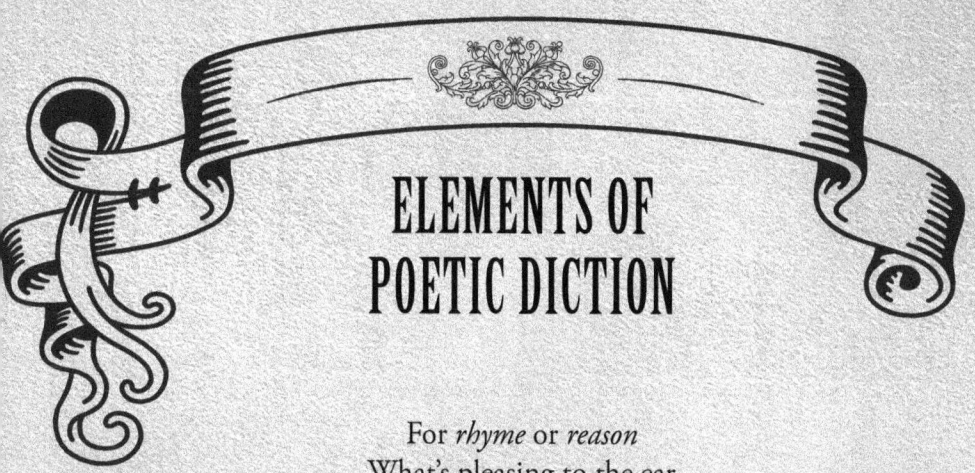

ELEMENTS OF
POETIC DICTION

For *rhyme* or *reason*
What's pleasing to the ear
Sounds incredibly austere
For profiled words
A clear conviction
Infers an unknown scholar's
Versions of articulated life lessons
Were honorarily

Placed alongside
Prevalent inscribed poem titles
Highlighted
A branded composition's
Emotional grace
Eternally welcomes
Surpassed unscripted verses
Through windows

Opened for rainbow overtones
Forever embracing
A beckoned pen's
Lifelike ink
Crowns a *finished* and *scripted* acquisition's
Known literary
Archived and *Canvassed*
Elements Of Poetic Diction

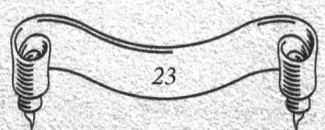

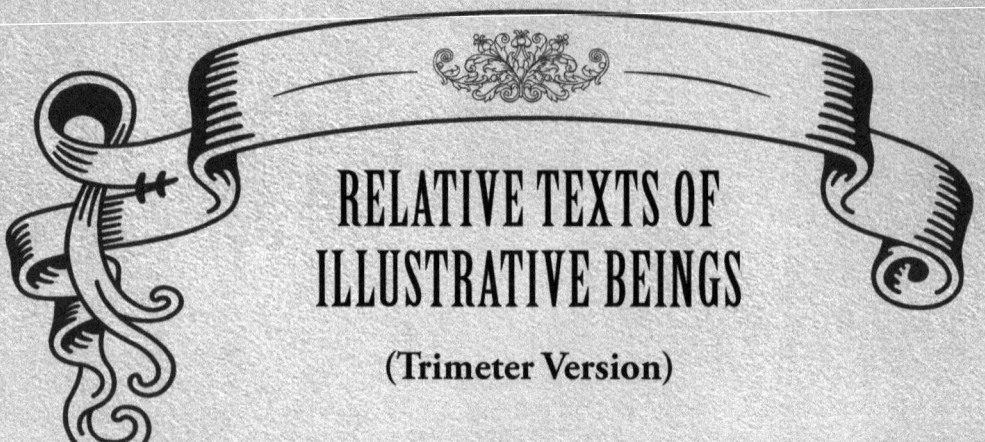

RELATIVE TEXTS OF ILLUSTRATIVE BEINGS

(Trimeter Version)

Messages of promise
Are often found hidden
Behind faded streaks of
Profound ink seen on vast
Pages characterized
For making replicas

Graced hieroglyphics were
Priceless images made
Memorable enough
For unfeigned worthiness
Celebrated yearly
As ***Relative Texts Of Illustrative Beings***

AN IN-DEPTH MYSTIQUE

Upon layers of
Viewed figurative speech
An In-Depth Mystique
Surfaced

A messaged creativity
Rarely encountered by readers
Seeking an acquired taste
Within designed text pages

Sought after in the night-light
Of conscious curiosity
Seated near their
Place for refuge reading

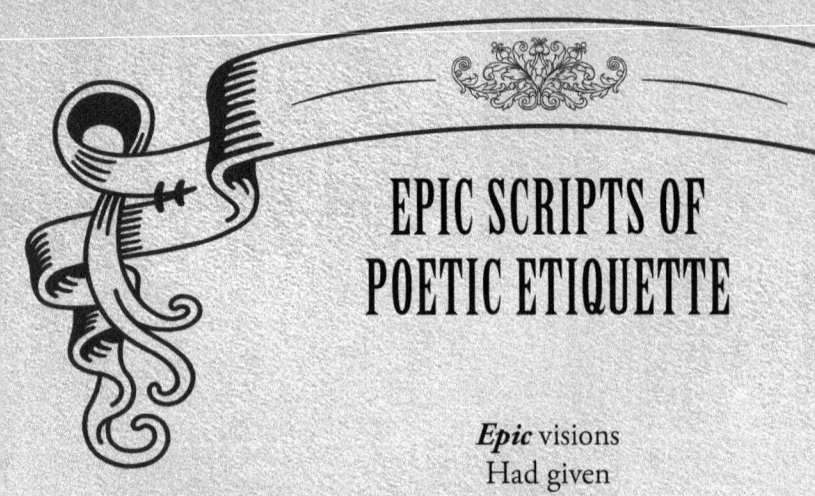

EPIC SCRIPTS OF
POETIC ETIQUETTE

Epic visions
Had given
Elaborate
Driven thoughts
A cue
To embark upon
Reflective
Yet

Priceless
Affluent excerpts
From a poet's
Hieroglyphic brush
Forever actualized
On cover art pages
Viewed within
Scripts Of Poetic Etiquette

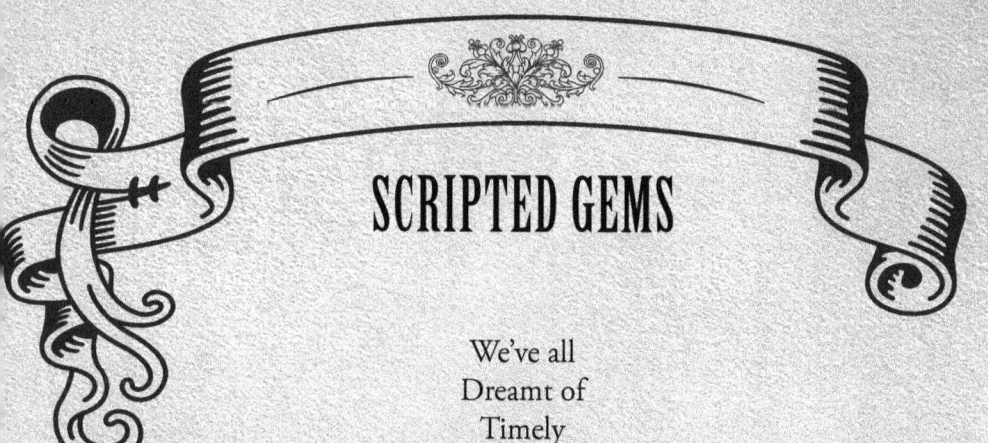

SCRIPTED GEMS

We've all
Dreamt of
Timely
Special
Places

Where white
Motioned
Quicksand
Had formed
Imaged
Mirages

Into
Lasting
Clouds seen
Drifting
Beyond
Our five
Senses
Upon
The End
Point of vague horizons
Lies a reassuring skyline
Where clouds of **Scripted** dreams
Forever relate to the **Gems** of each individual's written destiny

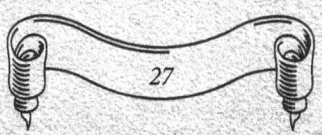

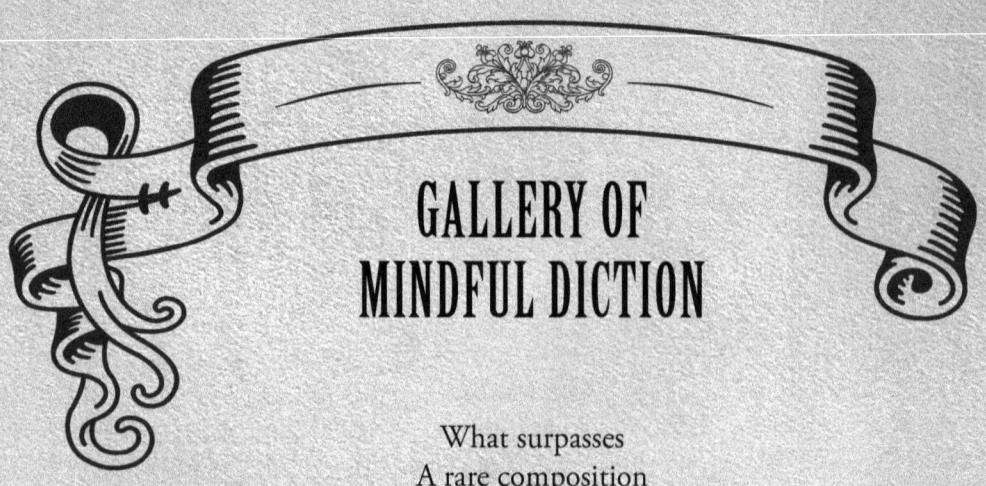

GALLERY OF
MINDFUL DICTION

What surpasses
A rare composition
Exhibit?
Engraved as

Being a display
Mutually inclined
To portray
Destined words belonging
On A Written Wall Of Inscriptions**

Envisioned
From a penned artistry
Built a literary shrine
Succeeded vastly
Before premiering
In its own divine
Prediction birthed a heartfelt
Gallery Of Mindful Diction

RELIC MASTERPIECES

Testing the sands of time
Themed messages
Often comply
With intrinsic values
Of found *Relic Masterpieces*

Encased in burial chests
These rare treasures
Are valued
In a class of their own
As known cherished keepsakes

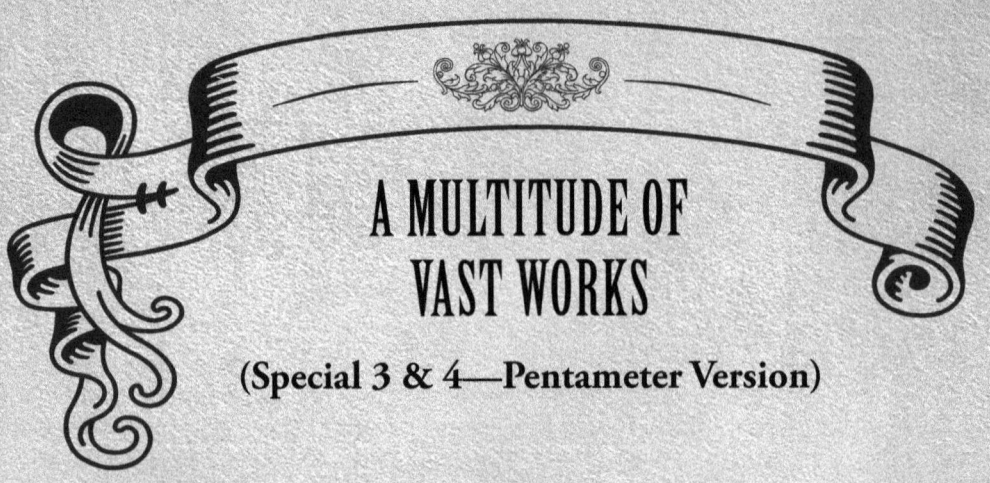

A MULTITUDE OF VAST WORKS

(Special 3 & 4—Pentameter Version)

A widespread
Aura meets
With topics
Blanketing
A written
Mural scene
Relating
More and *More*
To diverse
Viewpoints seen

Beyond the
Hemisphere
Represent
Purposeful
Yet to Be
Possible
Scholastic
Allure was
Pure enough
For an eye

Color shade
Welcomed man's
Steady-framed
Mindedness
Opened a
Windowpane
Upholding
Supported
Visions for
_Unveiling Thy True Self_* as **_A Gifted Mystique_***

Will spark all
_Meaningful Dawned Tomorrows_*
Within pondered psyches
Who're thirsting
For **_A Multitude Of Vast Works_**

A COMMEMORATIVE ESSENCE

A branded value
Seal of approval
Cleverly authenticated
With fitted ideals
Brushed upon

Paintings of resurgence
Forever birthed
A widespread
Scholastic
Reputation

Where ranging
Sacred carvings
Have stood
The test of time
Symbolically

These treasures inscribed
On outdated walls
Spanning volumes of traced brilliance
Stressed
A Commemorative Essence

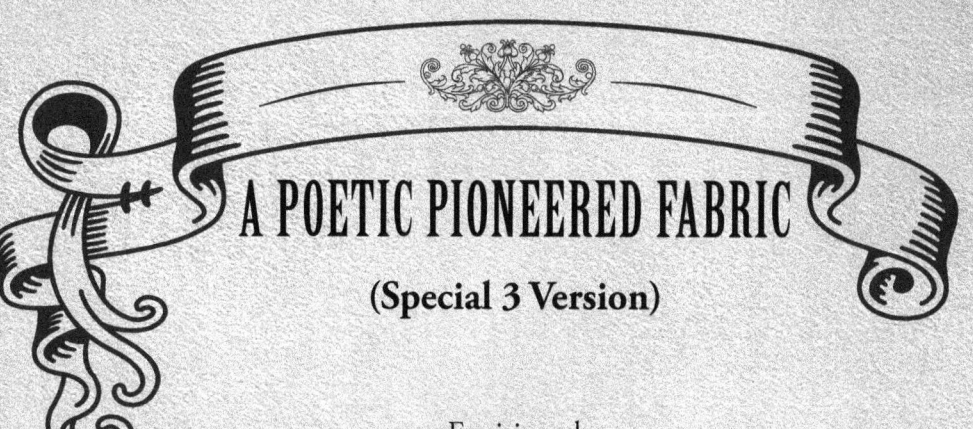

A POETIC PIONEERED FABRIC

(Special 3 Version)

Envisioned
Comprised words
Encompass
A binding
Quilt's sewing
Needled thread
Mirroring
Eventful
Images
Remembered
To uplift
Unified
Cultural
Diction views
Were built to
Last as their
Preserved seen

Fluency
Predicted
Twenty-six
Letters of
Written classed
Magic were
Tailored by
An unknown
Scholar who

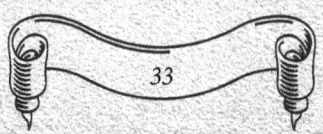

Claimed to show
Creative
Basis for
A visioned
Poetic
Pioneered
Fabric of
Expressed choice

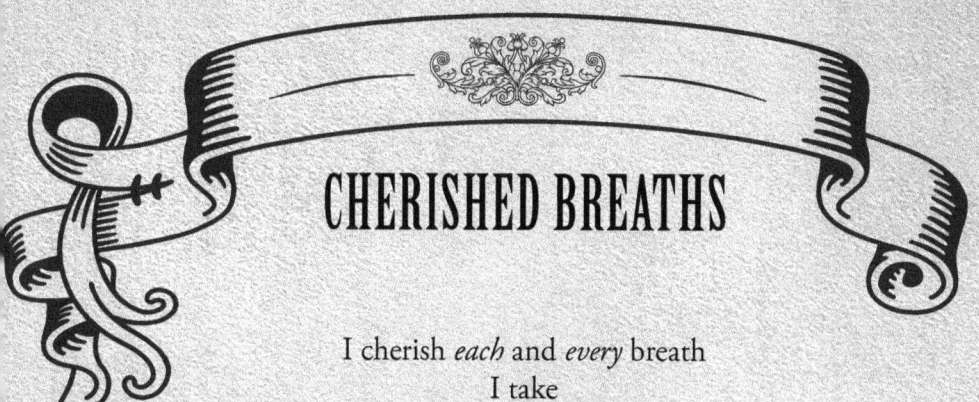

CHERISHED BREATHS

I cherish *each* and *every* breath
I take
As I *rise* and *rest*
Every day while
Making my way through the vagueness mist
Of false pretense
On all accounts

Which I've experienced during
My quest
To maintain substantiated graces
Seeing vast *faces* and *places*
After *each* and *every* moment
There's never stillness
It's hard to *predict* and *witness*

All of life's forecasts
For what lies ahead of my path
My lungs *expand* and *restrict*
The airways
I need to take in a precious
Gas called air
To help me share

Gifts of prized penmanship
With all well-wishers
Where my words reflect
All the **Cherished Breaths**
I've been blessed to take in retrospect
To life's travels
While being human

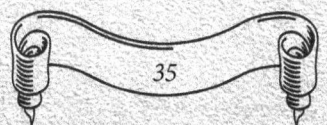

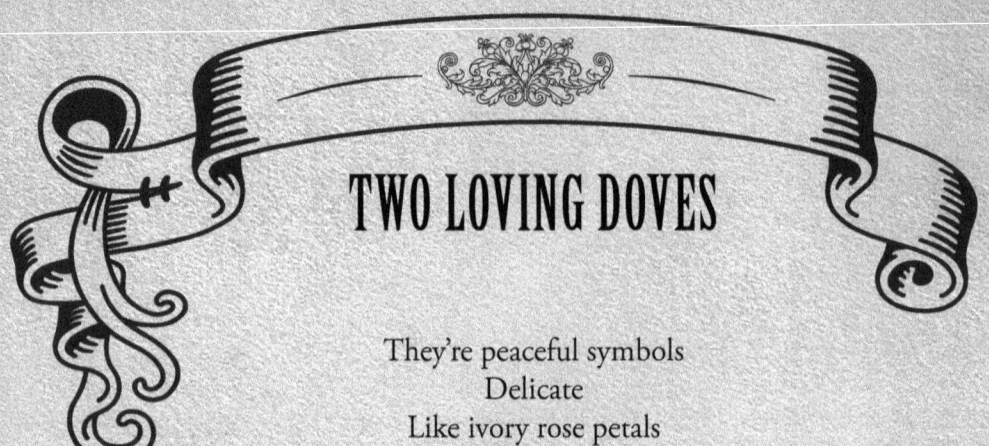

TWO LOVING DOVES

They're peaceful symbols
Delicate
Like ivory rose petals
Existing to preserve
Life's defining true endeavor
Happiness and *Humility*
Held in each hand
Meant to be extended
As a loving gesture

For all eyes to see
Feathered divinity
Remains to be
A stepping stone
For fulfilling an unwavering peace
Within the souls of *troubled hearts* and *dreams*
As they were lifted
To spread their wings
They flew away

Reminding us as human beings
To live graciously
One can only appreciate
This honorary scene from above
Flying in the clouds
Were **Two Loving Doves**
Together happily ever after
Depicted harmonious unions
Are always possible with *Faith* and *God's* relational blessings

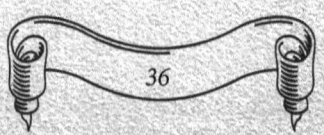

THE COPING WILLOWS

Shades of relief reside
Underneath a soothing leaf tree
As the ruined world
Criticizes and *Critiques*
Individual advocacy
Real breezes of adapted reality
Had whisked away
Governed heartbeats
From our souls

Free will committee
As vowed serendipity took over
It basked in the shadows
Momentarily as
Daylight called forth
Pristine
Serenity feathers
Fell from the sky
Into a sacred temple

Sets the stage
For ruined skeptics
Needing to *feel* and *hear*
Acceptance for why
Comfort's welcomed embrace
Chose eternal peace
As a foreground for beckoned transformative
Streams of assured promises depicted
The Coping Willows

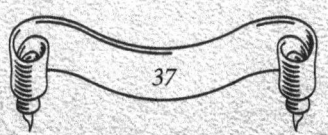

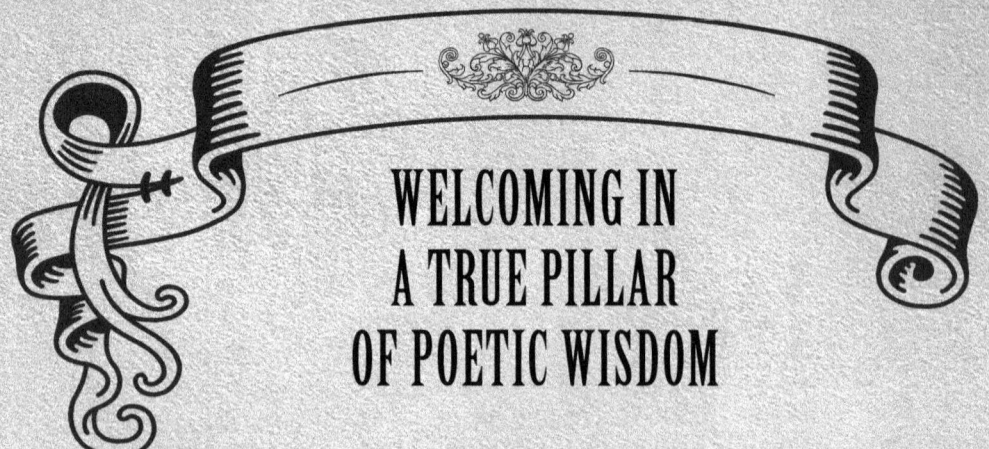

WELCOMING IN A TRUE PILLAR OF POETIC WISDOM

There's a time
When wisdom
Must find us
In order to rely
On our vowed conscious efforts
For *success* and *survival*
Of the contrived character
Lying dormant
Within all of our motives

Toward an effort
For viewing an inscription
Of poetic genius
Alongside a distinctive seen pillar
Outside the confines of our wisdom temple
Suggesting why
We should befriend charisma
In order to become an intellectual advocate for
Welcoming In A True Pillar Of Poetic Wisdom

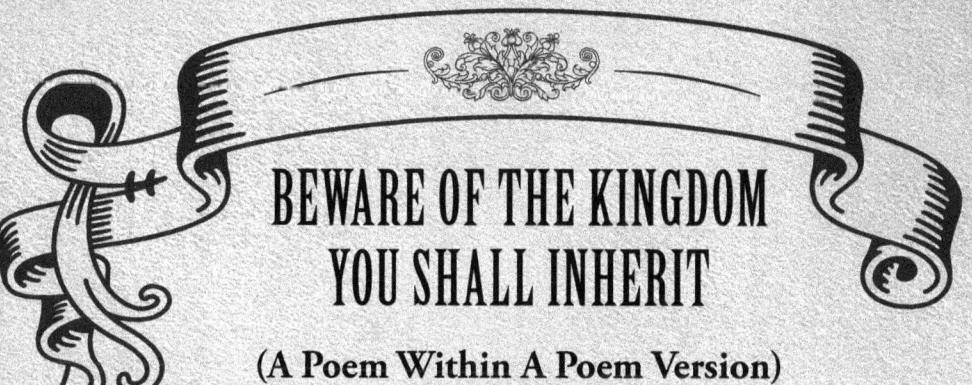

BEWARE OF THE KINGDOM YOU SHALL INHERIT

(A Poem Within A Poem Version)

(*Italicized Print Is The Second Poem*)

Your evolved *parents*
Took the loving *time*
To initiate your *induction*
Into a special
Heredity Kingdom Of Sorts
Deeming you as
Their prestigious prince or princess
Bearing a contemporaneous last name
Within the royal family court
Where ruling *power*
To profit and export *from* bartered *wisdom*
Transcends the solidarity
Reticent to a structured *governing order*
Was bearing more *light to a sight*
Of the king's ingeniously made
Fort castle's *lowering draw bridge close*
Inside the courtyard
An evident throne will reign now
Over every peasant
Yet ***Beware Of The Kingdom You Shall Inherit***
Without merit
A crumbling empire
Cannot withstand
Disloyal *subjects*
Breaking a chain of command

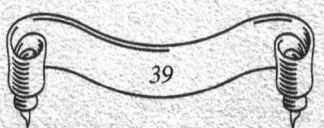

Represented by a pure *bloodline*
Of known *recipients*
Who'll keep the royal court's wheels
Turning to a point
Where *respect* and *recognition*
Will forever remain synonymous
In respect to the preceding
King and Queen's vision
Of *a prosperous* royal assembly and a *generational*
Non-transgressional *law-abiding kingdom*

WHEN WILL TIME
EVER STAND STILL

When Will Time Ever Stand Still
The lasting thrill
To achieve this
Would complete
The realization to never retreat

When opportunity presents itself
No one else
Has the power to halt the pendulum
Like a praised telekinetic medium
Feeling the rush

Expressively was made
Real behind a podium
Addressing the public
Within a golden symposium
Since their chosen spoken message

Had always been used
For finding the answer to why and
When Will Time Ever Stand Still
For only the positive benefits pertaining to sound free will
And not evil

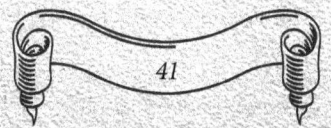

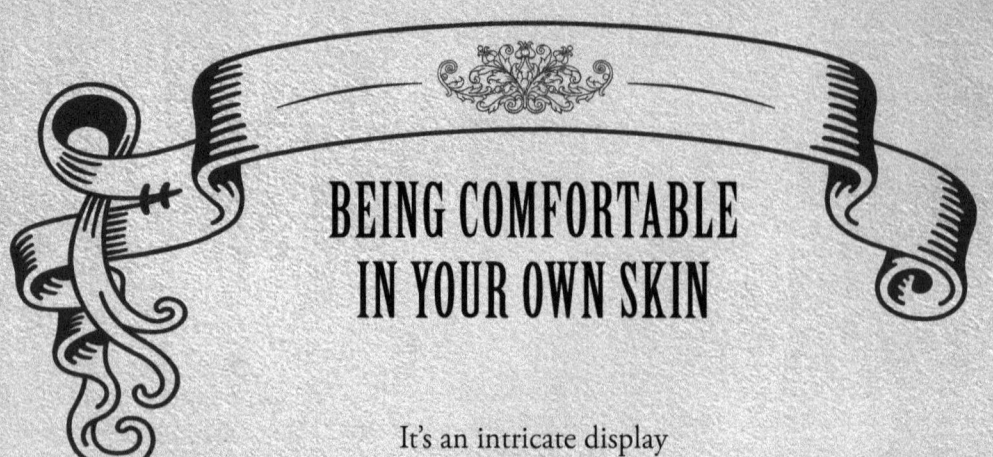

BEING COMFORTABLE
IN YOUR OWN SKIN

It's an intricate display
Where facial features
Convey
Dispositions

More intriguing per se
As the next complimentary face
Reassures you why it's a special grace
To share a rare distinctive

Living look to be
Featured and *Profusely* used
To bridge communicative barriers
Varying in *texture*, *pigmentation* and *tone*

Why condemn *emphasized* and *personalized* differences
When everyone wants to *share* and *win*
This relished experience called
Being Comfortable In Your Own Skin

WELCOMING THE COURSE OF IMMINENT CHANGE

(Octameter Version 3)

The brush of yesterday disappeared into a foray of
Forgotten relational ties had advised us as to why the
Wind had blown past our seen descriptiveness
For some time now we've come

To realize the daze of our true selves will forever shine since we've
Believed a auspicious day's dawning shows us
Often why we've conveyed ***Welcoming The***
Course Of Imminent Change

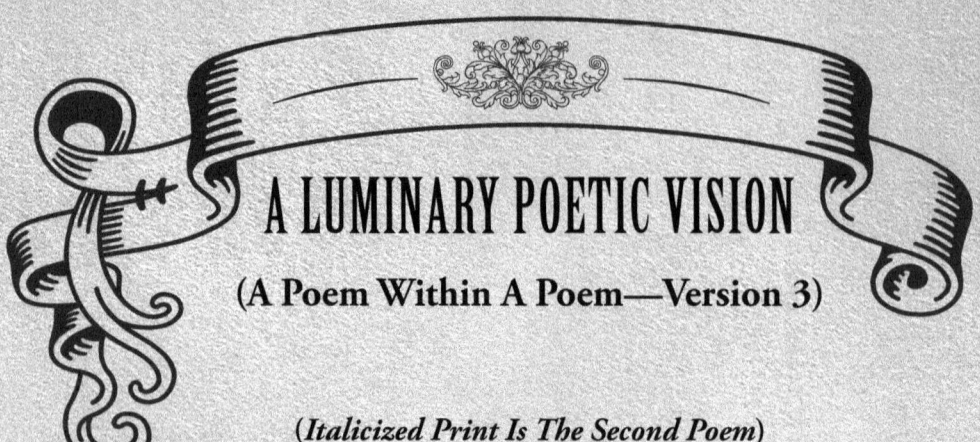

A LUMINARY POETIC VISION

(A Poem Within A Poem—Version 3)

(*Italicized Print Is The Second Poem*)

Orchestrating *a clairvoyant* and *figurative*
Broadening scheme thereby
Uplifting fellow *poetry lovers*
Into believing anything in life *is possible*
Once they've chosen
To *become visionaries*
In *their own* written reich
For an *honorary plight*
Of grand personalized *significance*
Will help crown *them to be poetic kings* and *queens*
Within the public eye
By sparking enough real
Attention toward
A well-*deserved nomination*
For their induction
Into every esteemed *library*
Across a newly defined and *revived*
Poetic Renaissance Nation
Favoring a literary genre
In need of vibrant *poetic pioneers*
Who will forever *pledge allegiance*
Toward fortifying
This special rare spectacle
In the making for years to come
Now deemed *as*
A Luminary Poetic Vision
Being *cherished* for generations

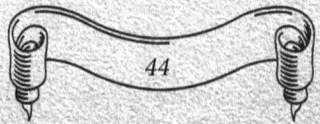

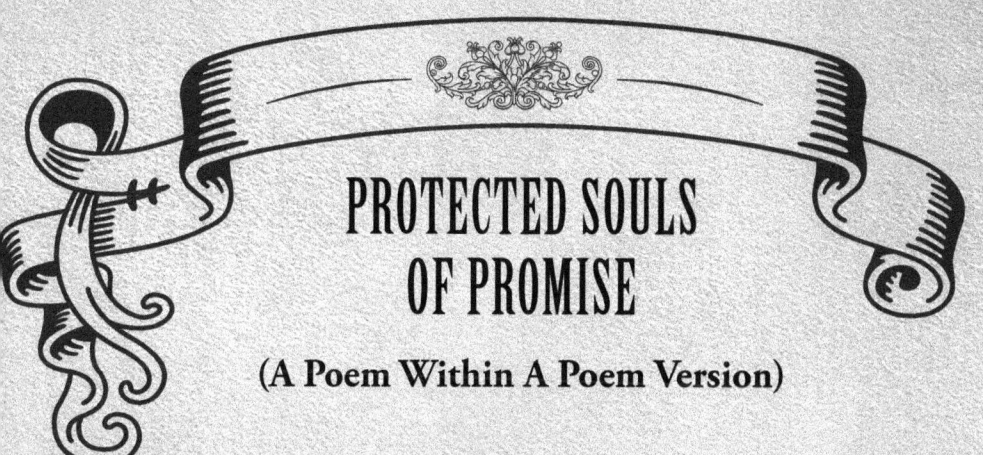

PROTECTED SOULS
OF PROMISE

(A Poem Within A Poem Version)

(*Italicized Print Is The Second Poem*)

The *Storms* of uncertainty
Have no memory
Within bound minds a clued
Destiny is observing from
A conservatory of affairs
Where society's antagonistic
Turbulent *Daily whispers*
Declare finality
As a curse
Denying *Budding potential*
Before it's
A procreated verse
In this trivial world
Calamity
Never *plays* fair
Without a *care*
Where?
In the midst of travesties
Is *the key?*
To unlock *paradise's*
Luminary spokesman
Who *will* forever *unveil*
The *eternal lists*
Of all future
Protected Souls Of Promise

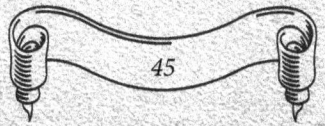

MEANINGFUL DAWNED TOMORROWS

(Octameter Version 3)

Ceremonial rays of sunshine vividly interplay as
Perceived *Meaningful* landscape monologues
Pulsated within the hearts
Of beloved observers who pictured jubilation in luck with
Scenic signs near a personal revelation's balcony style
View unveiled written clues where a lasting
Rainbow's gleeful message
Mirrored in the air *Dawned* fluorescent
Flares from *Tomorrows* graced sky
By far calligraphic cumulus clouds found telepathy as
Soliloquies befittingly spelled aloud profound vows later
Revealed what's yet to come from mankind's unbridled future's past

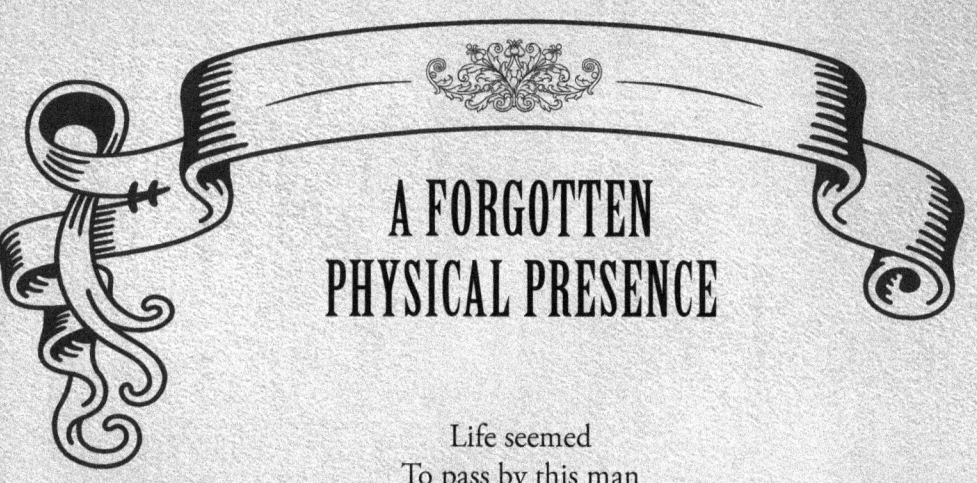

A FORGOTTEN
PHYSICAL PRESENCE

Life seemed
To pass by this man
Who tried fitting in
As an outcast

With the laws of the land
Only to have
Society's conformity rug pulled
Right out from under him

What else could he do?
Since no one really had a clue
Why he existed
With such a pure heart of graciousness

It's a shame
These types of people
In life become
A Forgotten Physical Presence

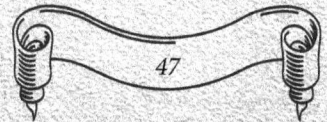

LIVE TO BECOME
A LIVING MYTH

Can it be
Possible to see
A living myth
In its entirety?
Passing through life
Endowed to ignite the flames

Of our imaginations
Beyond disbelief
Mostly everyone got lost in a moment
Which had surfaced
Within every mind
Who loved to befriend speculation

At all costs
The loss of obviousness
Remains the real gift
For anyone who candidly desires
The privilege to *Live To
Become A Living Myth*

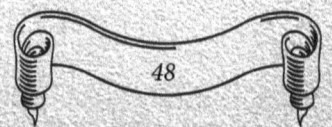

NEVER FORGET
WHERE YOU COME FROM

Never Forget Where You Come From
Because
The way you were raised
Will keep you safe for the rest of your days
As the sun *rises*
And *sets*
The course during your life's journey
Will not divert from
Staying true to your own pledged personal requests
For obtaining prevalence

Will become solidified
Beyond concrete while not existing in vain
Foreboding what could happen within society's social terrain
Maintains the perspective needed to
Feel *grateful* and *blessed*
As the days to fulfill your conquest
To obtain an edged meaningful objective
Remains not obstinate

But progressive
As you try
To reach the finish line
Becoming the champion
Of your proposed destiny
A designated door will open
So your fateful time-lined reality will unfold
At the right designated time
In your life

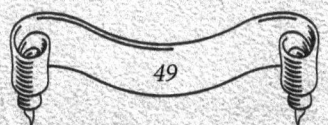

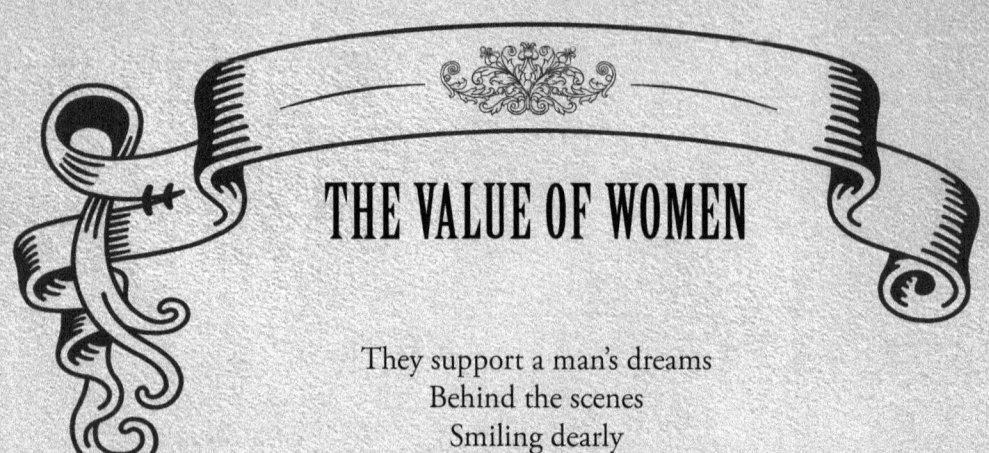

THE VALUE OF WOMEN

They support a man's dreams
Behind the scenes
Smiling dearly
As cadences for their affection
Lie within the attraction
Of what they see in
The gentleman of their dreams
Claiming to love
Their knight in shining armor by
Backing every cause he stands for

Sharing their *love* and *tenderness*
Like a charmer with allure
Don't underestimate
The Value Of Women
If not for them there would be no more men
To *defend* and *honor* them with their bravery
Lovingly and *Respectfully*
With intent of preserving their images
As special caregivers
Within our whole society

AN UNFOLDING ETERNITY

The fate of
One spirited soul
Left a lasting mark
Symbolically toward
Spiritual preservation

Within a dominion
Where darkness consumed
Ruled daylight hours
Perpetually by
An Unfolding Eternity

YOUR SOUL'S
PEACEFUL GARDEN

Whispering springs of redemption
Were heard like rare birds chirping
A soothing soliloquy
Promoting refuge serenity
After our lifetime's past
Has run its course
Beyond the limelight

An undeniable impact
Had been felt
As a generation of skeptics'
Invaluable wisdom
Dared and *Cared*
To inform the uninformed
Of what's yet to come

As long as you follow
The reign of your heart's desires
You will ultimately
Find entrances
Into the authentic
Presence of
Your Soul's Peaceful Garden

UNVEILING THY TRUE SELF

This transparent veil
Most of us use
As a shield toward
Life's criticisms
By other human beings

Propositions
Nerve-stricken tendencies
Within ourselves
There's a rare selfishness
To protect

The reputational health
On the surface
Of our relational composure
It's a wealth
In need of a full disclosure

To no one else
Unless vanity pertains to merit
Uncovering intent
On the grounds of
Unveiling Thy True Self

AN UNDISCLOSED PREVIEW

(Original—Revised Version)

Being away
From what my heart
Desires the most
Will only wet
A dry well
Of self-expression

Servicing the thirsts of true fans
Who believe in their favorite poet's
Writing hand
Now on the verge
Of unfolding
What's yet to come

Within the mesmerizing context
Of a scarce
One-of-a-kind narration
Now on display
In full view as
An Undisclosed Preview

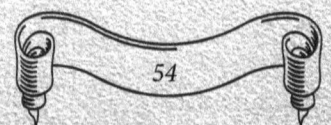

A GIFTED MYSTIQUE

People were
In awe
Of this charismatic
Individual
Who starred in

A cinematic disposition
That now
Graced the viewing
Of their life's story
As a mystified public noticed

Everyone this person
Came in contact with
Experienced
A life-changing epiphany
Near the depths of every candid soul

All personal fortunes
Were vividly foretold
As *A Gifted Mystique* unfolded
The world's future
Became known

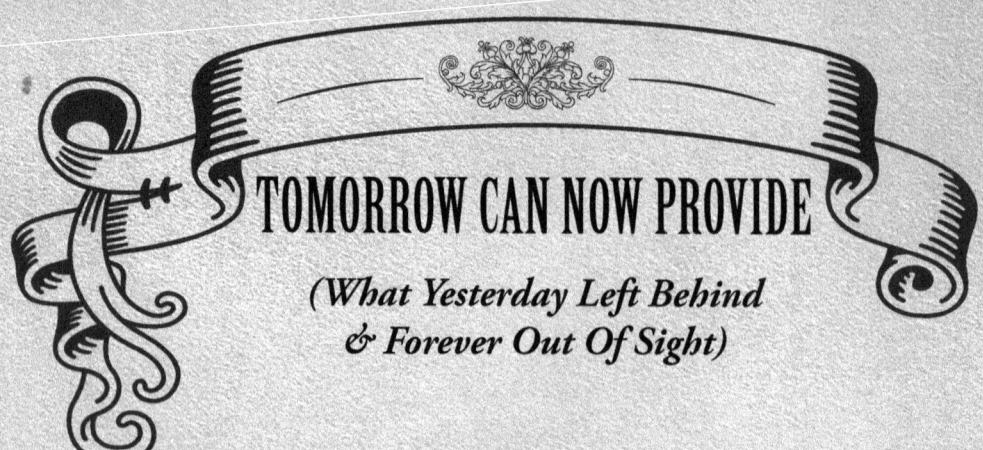

TOMORROW CAN NOW PROVIDE

(What Yesterday Left Behind
& Forever Out Of Sight)

It's amazing
What we yearn for
In a twenty-four-hour period
Zeal-type dreams
For ourselves

Are often
Left undone
After reality's divinity
Failed to include them upon resurgence
Since our *chosen* and *envisioned* future

Remains inadvertently destined to be
An invisible hand of shifting influence
Making aforementioned found treasures
More promising than
The near present

Ever made possible
Gives life to
A purposeful view of optimism
Can only openly dispel
Negativity's grip

Within our emotional consciousness
Once we finally realize
The vision for partaking what
Tomorrow Can Now Provide
(What Yesterday Left Behind & Forever Out Of Sight)

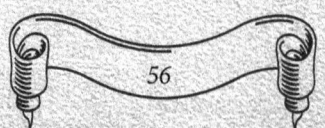

FROM DARKNESS TO DAYLIGHT AS THE BURIAL MOUNDS REPLIED

From Darkness To Daylight
The burial mounds
Were crying out
Where have you been?
The world ended a long time ago
I said
I couldn't let go
Of this wonderful privilege called life
So I hid
When the apocalypse had commenced

Now I'm the sole survivor
Who can be present
To live in peace
The Burial Mounds Replied
You ignoramus
Dying is why you have to live
You missed your chance to experience
A greater privilege
I asked
What could that possibly be?

The burial mounds replied
A known worry-free eternity
Without a body
Everyone will have the same shining spiritual bright light
No more malice and no more strife against the flesh
The burial mounds attested
Who in the world disillusioned your own thought process?
I said
My own self
Cause I was scared of experiencing death

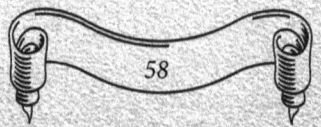

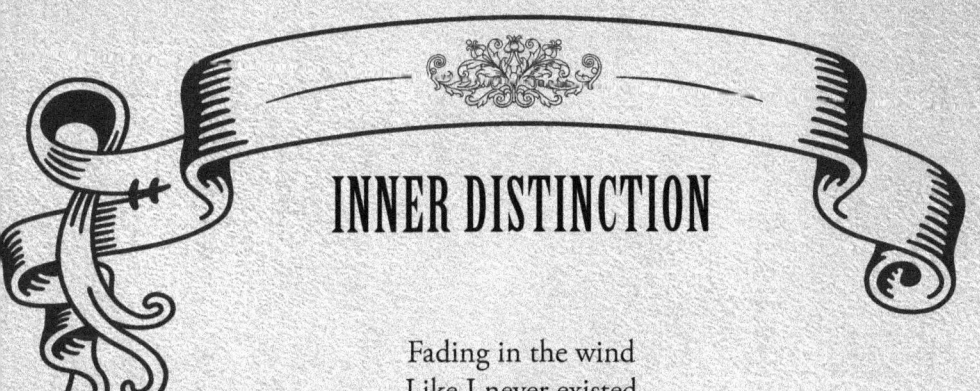

INNER DISTINCTION

Fading in the wind
Like I never existed
This gift for coveted diction
Is relevant evidence
An ***Inner Distinction***

Will be in my own right
For the extent of a purpose
Refined within a revealed structured outline
An unknown mortal time line
Became a sought mystery

So future generations
Would look it up in engraved text to find
A dignified scholar
Who made an emphatic impact
To supply his best admirers with

Transcending poetry that could help solidify
Their desired character in life
So they can become model beings
During their lifetime as well as in the afterlife's
Realm of changed spirits

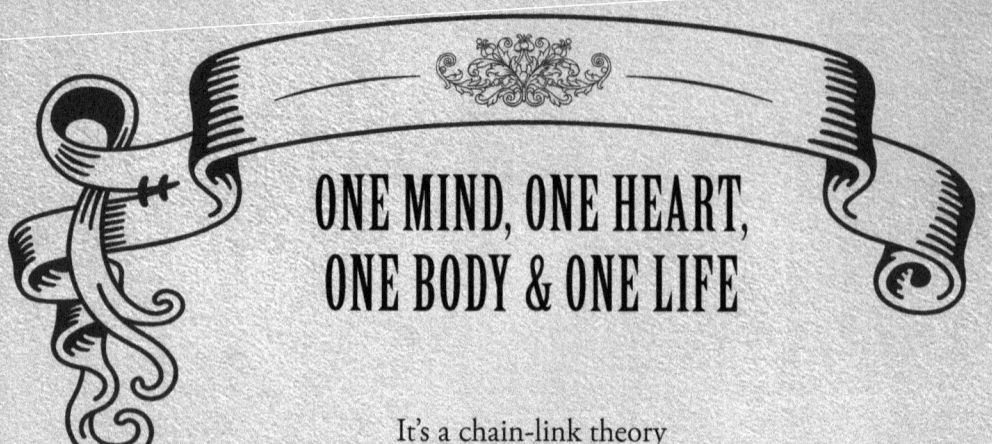

ONE MIND, ONE HEART, ONE BODY & ONE LIFE

It's a chain-link theory
In hindsight
One Mind, One Heart, One Body & One Life
Signals what truly embodies
A temporal physique

Moving to the heartbeat
Of one's desired journeys through
A world of unpredictable natures
Meaningful forecasts of intricacy
Curiously have sparked

A core fascination
Within the minds
Of every God-given
Earthly existing face
May only explain

Why shared testimonials
From a faithful podium
Could shed light upon
Every heard individual's
Cross Bearing and *Chosen*

Lifelong purposes
Once they've completed
Their own travels
Down a desired relevant road
Of self-fulfilled credentials

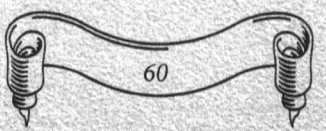

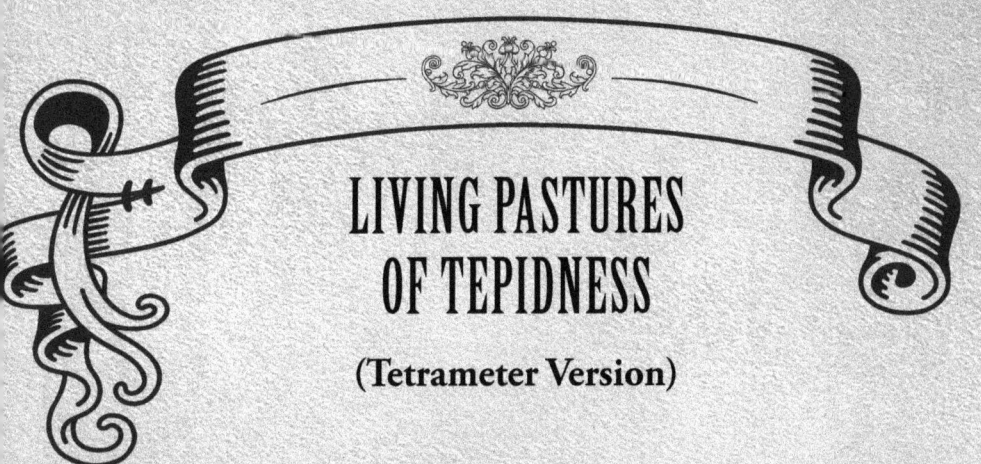

LIVING PASTURES
OF TEPIDNESS

(Tetrameter Version)

It's a welcoming of open
Arms where alarms do not exist
Only after ongoing and
Smiling faces persist in grand
Friendliness by giving calling
Cards of endearment to distant
Nonbelievers of a cultured
Truth meant to belittle common
Courtesy sets in motion a
Need to preserve prized legacies
Fathomed from the hearts of threshold
Contemporaries within the
Living Pastures Of Tepidness

HONORED CAMARADERIE

Whatever happened to those rare days?
When it was fun
To embrace your peers
Without fears of a double cross
Where genuine innocence
Seemed to be forever in a day

As friendly decency
Was always *angelic* and *automatic*
Yet *our time* and *celestial presence*
Always sends us on different paths
Toward self-fulfillment as it
Remains cataclysmic

To vast intellects
Who've never understood
Self-vulnerability
Since they've never been dispelled
From an advised case of
Honored Camaraderie

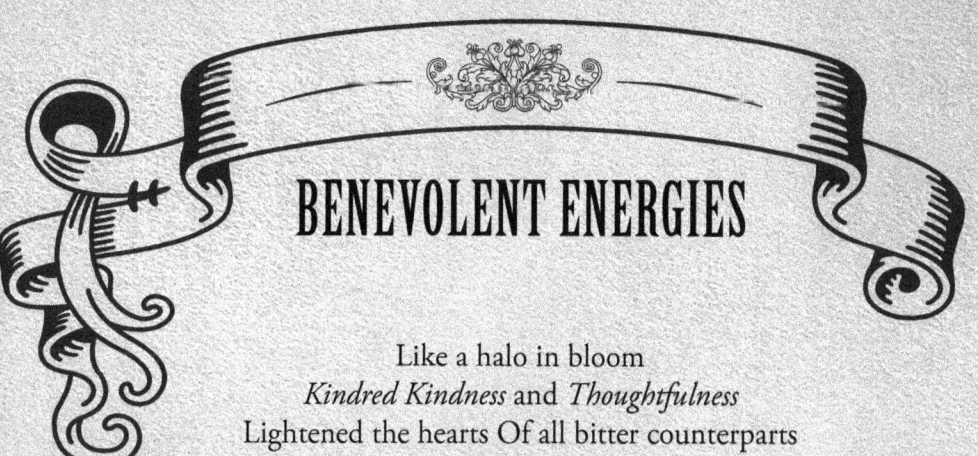

BENEVOLENT ENERGIES

Like a halo in bloom
Kindred Kindness and *Thoughtfulness*
Lightened the hearts Of all bitter counterparts
Who were on A jealousy quest

To *siege* and *beset* Peace from noteworthy lives Presently
in harmony with Private impinging elegies
Exist as valued
Benevolent Energies

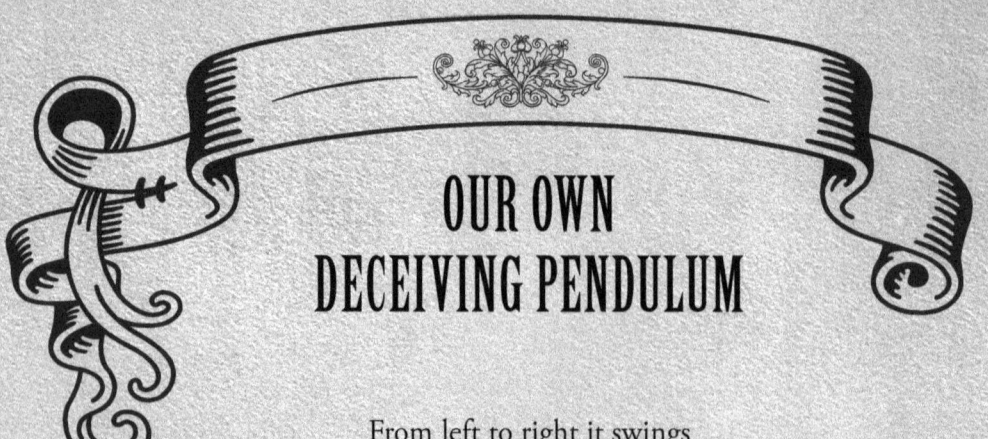

OUR OWN
DECEIVING PENDULUM

From left to right it swings
Forecasting probable
Visions and *Dreams*
Of a phased reality momentarily
Our *Wants* and *Desires*
Are claimed

Falsely fortified
Since an unwilling convergence
Chose to surface its graces
Within our subliminal compliances
Newly birthed benign depths
Once mirrored

Wishful envisioned metaphysics
Resting within our subconscious
Lies an unknown brain wave rhythm
Viable to those in tune with themselves
Discreetly in disguise as
Our Own Deceiving Pendulum

CLEVERLY WRITTEN MONTAGE

Sequences of written stanzas
Have unfolded
Like a hieroglyphic's storyline

Molded into a clay-designed
Figurine within its shaped entirety
Before being *housed* and *displayed*

Within a poetic gallery's
Hall Of **Cleverly Written Montage**
So all admirers can see

A relative embroidery
Of a *scripted* and *sculptured* made
Masterpiece in the making

Creates
Perfected corridors
Of brilliance

Special Edition

(Bonus Material)

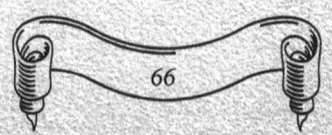

B-POET

B-poet is a Hieroglyphic archaeologist and aspiring American poet who loves to create memorable poetry for every adoring fan who loves to appreciate the written art of written self-expression. He originates from Indianapolis, Indiana; His passion for poetry and writing remains to be a prime catalyst for his own poetic expertise. His poetry has been showcased internationally as BK in a poetry book titled *International Who's Who of Poetry 2012*. His poetry has also been featured as BK in the United States as well by Eber & Wein Publishing which includes these poetry compilation books. *American Poet, From A Window: Wistful Thoughts, Best Poets of 2014 – 2016, and Who's Who in American Poetry 2016 – 2017*. His hobbies include reading, writing, listening to music and traveling. He can also be followed on twitter at www.twitter.com/newfacepoet.

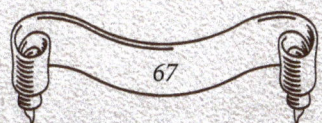

B-POET

Origins of the Lost Poetic Archives from an Unknown Scholar

Who has discovered an invaluable collection of written artifacts within encrypted Egyptian burial vaults during their archaeological trip in 2015? B-poet, a Hieroglyphic archaeologist and aspiring American poet, compellingly unveils the Origins of the Lost Poetic Archives from an Unknown Scholar alongside pillars, stop entrances and along walls inside an Egyptian pyramid just south of the Mediterranean Sea. During this historic unveiling he later decodes a hieroglyphic scroll found just behind an Egyptian Bronze Dog Statue right outside the entrance of our unknown scholar's possible tomb. The scroll's message which B-poet soon uncovers may enlighten mythical skeptics to ponder... Why the origins of these mysterious archives could only ever be made known to those who dare to seek out what truly lies within them?

CLICK TO BUY

ORIGINS OF THE LOST ARCHIVES

Welcome to the Origins of the Lost Poetic Archives from an Unknown Scholar my name is B-poet and I'll be your guide during this poetic expedition. It was a great honor to share with Authorhouse publishing what was hidden within these vast written archives back in 2015.

Around that time I was a cultural seeker searching for what lessons an Ancient Egyptian civilization could teach us today on how our present day society should be evolving. Culture, customs, and amazing hieroglyphic diction lead me to believe this unknown scholar meant a lot to his civilization thousands of years ago.

He left behind at least sixty poetic gems; The majority of them, I decoded, devolve deeply and stylistically into the written realms of spirituality, haiku, parable, love, death, chivalry, and even personal optimism.

When I arrived in Ancient Egypt back in 2015, I was very excited to search and uncover a legend from yesterday's past. It's quite rare to find such literary & hieroglyphic history. You have to be in the right place at the right time.

You can then be able to understand the impact of being a part of such history as if it were happening in the present. I always had that type of attitude when it comes to being a part of history. A historic trail of poetic genius is the best way to describe this book. Throughout my career this unknown scholar has fascinated the likes of myself along with today's generational writing community's curiosity as a whole.

As I furthered my journey through these vast archives, I noticed shades of hieroglyphic mastery along walls, inside burial vaults, up and down pillars, along detailed door frames & mantles, atop ceilings, and even

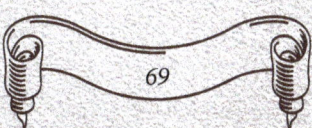

behind Egyptian Bronze Dog Statues where I found a hieroglyphic scroll which was written as a sacred living testament.

I further investigated and decoded what was written on this sacred living testament as it read: "Here a literary gateway lies before your very eyes. This sacred testament only bears true origins of the lost written poetic archives from an unknown scholar; His numerous written works will reveal an enchanting way of life that's in-store for those who've become very disenchanted with their own world and way of life in which they've supposedly become accustomed to."

The message itself stood out like an oracle sharing invaluable hieroglyphic wisdom to those seeking enlightenment. Also, there were many Egyptian symbols I had to decode yet what struck my imagination and curiosity the most is how the patterns of these poems were created along with a personal signature afterward. I often came across one unique symbol which read after being decoded B-K.

The numerous translations, B-K signatures, and symbols made me well aware that this unknown scholar had a major influence on his people and culture. His style of penmanship is what touched me the most. I'd never seen how a legendary Egyptian poet and writer could convey hieroglyphic diction in such a manner.

Realistically and by the nature of my findings there's no telling who this unknown scholar's ancestry traces back to. There's definitely no telling who's the present-day heir of this unknown scholar's bloodline for such rare and talented written artistry. It was oddly strange though he wasn't worthy enough to be placed in one of the many burial vaults I seen within these archives. In my next publication of findings hopefully I'll know and find out who's the present-day heir of such gifted hieroglyphic talents. There's a message worth searching for within every poem. Every titled poem traces back to the origins of this unknown scholar's treasured written scripts.

Each poem also represents a literary journey that's worth taking if you enjoy reading great poetry. I never imagined the depth of his creativity and expressive imagination were so vivid with inspirational promise. Yet out all his fascinating hieroglyphic poetry I did find an intriguing yet puzzling train of thought our unknown scholar had left behind.

I'm fascinated with the art of poetry but the third particular line in the poem "A Collaborative Touch (Pentameter Version)" is quite mysterious. As I further decoded this line on a standing pillar near the front of the archives it read "Attended a Being Comfortable In Your Own Skin." This line didn't quite favor the meter of the whole poem to me.

Yet there were only two possible conclusions which could make since in my mind. First, this line could've read "Knew Being Comfortable In Your Skin"; or second, it could've read "Attended a Vertigo Masquerade."

I wasn't able to find any more written hieroglyphics pertaining to this messaged mystery in order to solve it. On the other hand, I came to realize that maybe this line was just a preview for future poems to come by our unknown scholar and nothing more. I have to say it's quite an achievement being a part of Paperclips magazine. It's a dream come true to see my findings within these poetic archives are now exclusively surfacing so the public can experience them within this magazine for 2018.

Although I'm still in the process of identifying this unknown scholar, it's amazing how he's become an inspiration to me once I found his treasured diction. I later decided to read and follow the sacred living testament as a token of my appreciation for his artistry.

The lasting impact this literary hieroglyphic expedition and our unknown scholar have had on me over the years has been very humbling and monumental at the same time. I encourage everyone who's taken the time to read this article about *Origins of the Lost Poetic Archives of an Unknown Scholar* to go on your very own poetic adventure within these archives.

Discover and uncover the life changing diction that may influence and give meaning to all the curiosities you value in your own life. So, you can have the same enlightening experience as a take away from these poetic findings as I did. Thank you for reading, take care and God bless.

CLICK HERE TO BUY

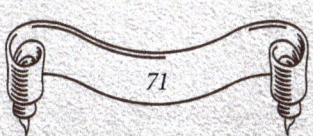

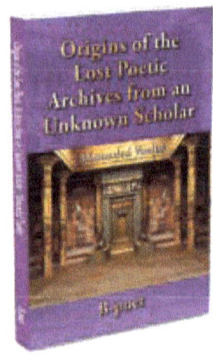

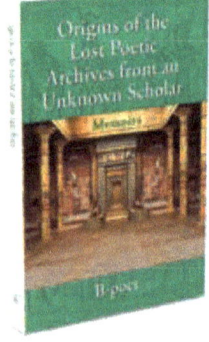

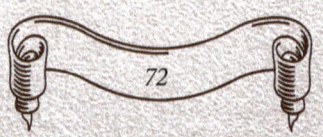

Special Edition

(Bonus Poems)

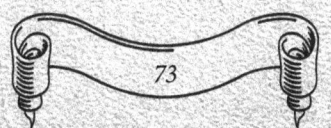

A CALAMITY UNCOMMON
TO MANKIND

Understanding the very nature of every calamity
Establishes a newfound reality
As time must progress to present
This discerning question to all men
Who search for *wisdom* and *blessings*

Within the curiosity of their souls inherited
Due to this questionable predetermined mortal curse

Am I ready to fill the shoes
Of a man who needs clues
To *pick* and *choose*
A course for my own life
Which I will later lose?

Stemming from the
Earthly elements were exposing
A Calamity Uncommon To Mankind

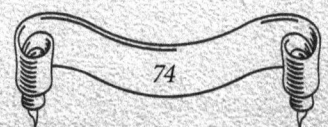

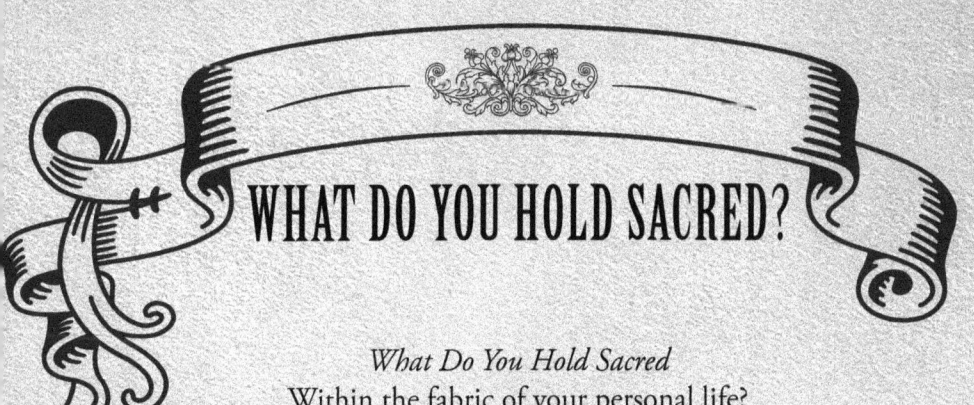

What Do You Hold Sacred
Within the fabric of your personal life?
Is it family?
Is it money?
Is it spirituality?

What about stretching out
Time's karmic influence
In relation to
Combating personal doubt
As the unknown

Sets the tone for
What You Hold Sacred?
In contrast to meeting the needs
For fulfilling daily voids
That plague us all

As living personalities that are
Dying to grow
Toward reaching our destined potential
As mortals within
A corrupt world of misfortune

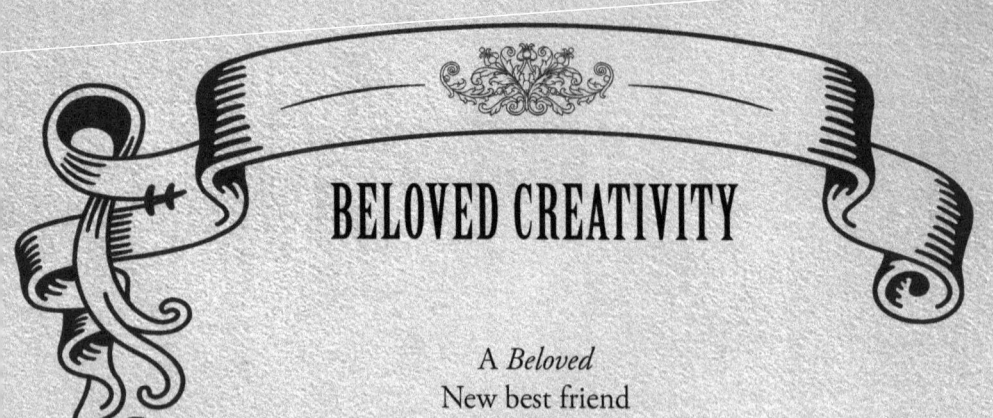

BELOVED CREATIVITY

A *Beloved*
New best friend
Named *Creativity*
Had me experience
An ever-changing freedom
To dream
Beyond reality's presence
Since hindsight remains to be
20/20
Creativity gave me
The inspiration to paint a perfect

Picture on a written canvass
Showed personal
Defined excellence
Within the social currents
Of a land bombarded by
Worldly events meant
To decline character values
Led by common people
Who chose not to understand
The belief in a vast underlying visionary Being called ***Beloved Creativity***

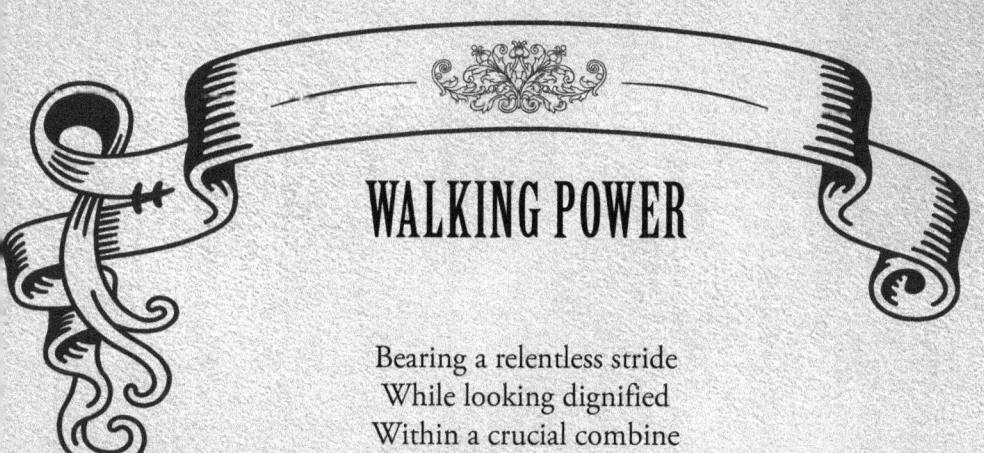

WALKING POWER

Bearing a relentless stride
While looking dignified
Within a crucial combine
At war with
The race against time

Each and *Every* step
Is enough influentially
To gratify the extent
Of a savored ***Walking Power***
Meant to triumph over

Any obstacle along
The pathway toward
All wayward graces
Life has on demand
For anyone

Who wanted to win
The race against the present
Refutable laws of the land
Were for us to follow despite
The conflict created by them for our souls

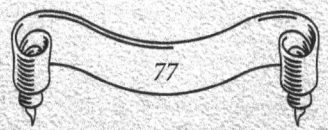

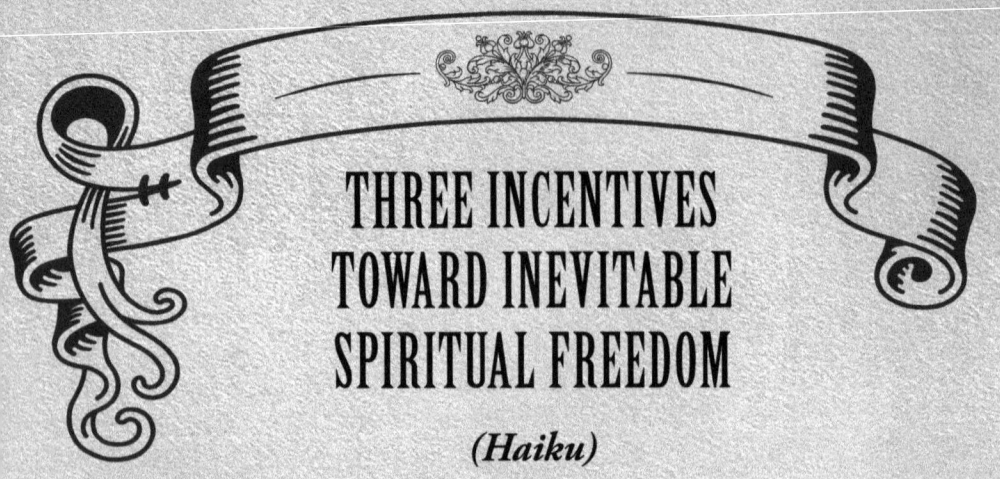

THREE INCENTIVES TOWARD INEVITABLE SPIRITUAL FREEDOM

(Haiku)

Our God hears all prayers
Believe a higher power
Will favor your cause

FOREVER TIMELESS

It's amazing to see
A written art
Shaping a microcosm
Of literary *minds* and *admirers*

From all walks of life
Into not forgetting why poetry
Will always remain engraved
In *libraries* and *honorary* texts

Of shelved inscripted classics
Deemed within a large prophetic
Poetic volume immensely titled
Forever Timeless

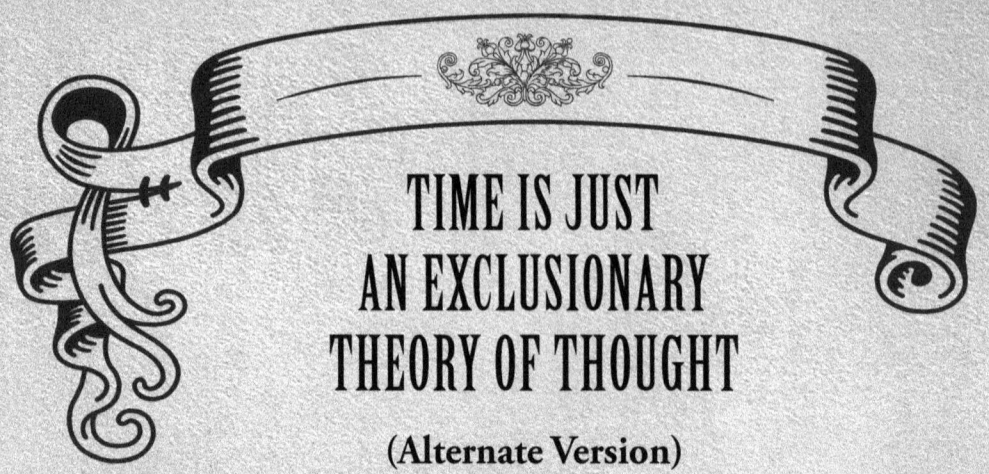

TIME IS JUST AN EXCLUSIONARY THEORY OF THOUGHT

(Alternate Version)

What's the significance
Of knowing that time
Is an anticipation
For what's yet to come
During a phase
In your life's tenure

What will be
Made known to the
Forefront of consciousness
Within everyone?
When time clearly reiterates
Every expectation

Within your mind to date
If said tomorrows are not promised
Then they will remain mysterious
Until daybreak resurfaces momentarily
Rekindling the innocence lost from our lives
Since *Time Is Just An Exclusionary Theory Of Thought*

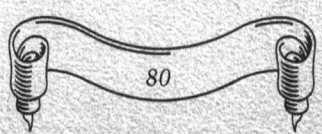

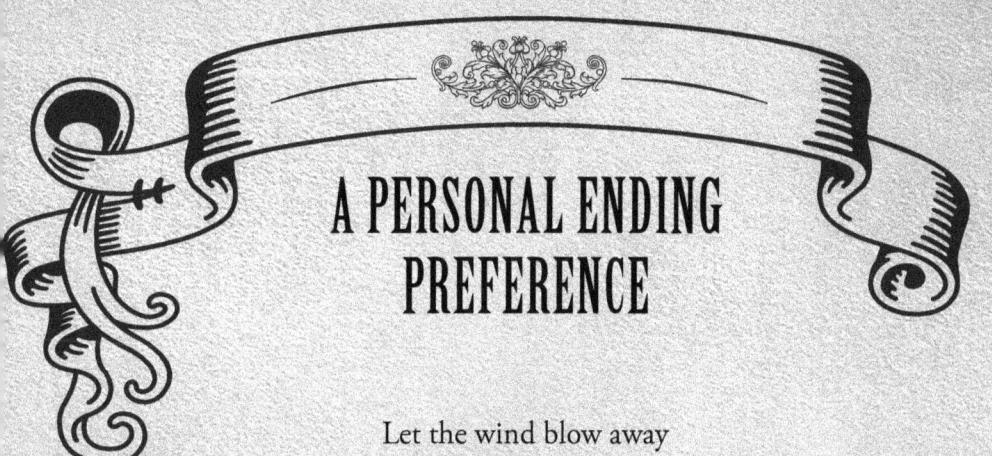

A PERSONAL ENDING
PREFERENCE

Let the wind blow away
My ashes to where
They've never been before
What's in store
For my remains

After this bountiful journey
Ends during the peaceful memorial of
A Personal Ending Preference
As serene as solace Comforting my soul

My contribution toward helping
The earth's ongoing display
Of civilization's obsession
With a greater tomorrow
Rather than cherishing

A better yesterday
Remained the forever in a day cause
Within vested minds
Of a *million* or *more* inhabitants
Who've benefited from my existence

Even after my tenure
Has passed away
With my own inhibitions making it through
The Hall Of Fame For Philanthropists
Who've blessed society as a whole

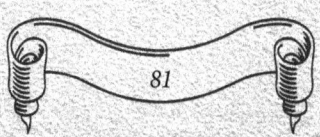

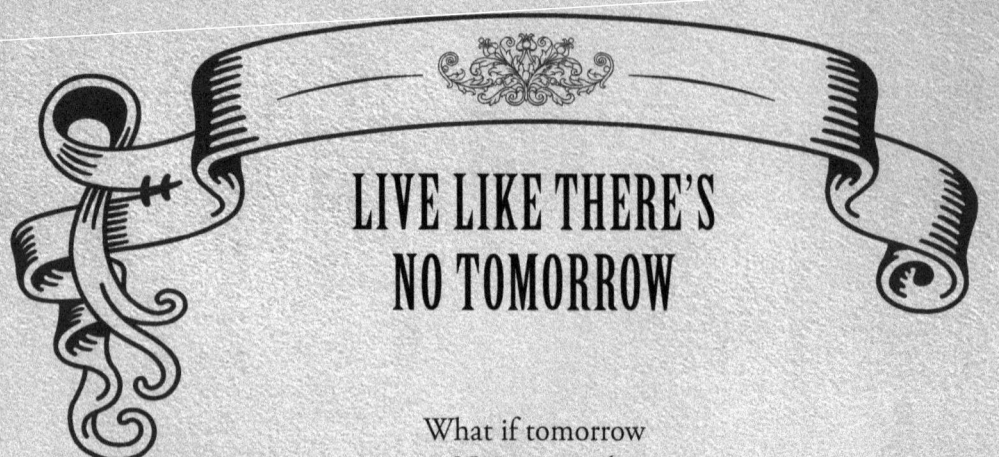

LIVE LIKE THERE'S
NO TOMORROW

What if tomorrow
Never existed
And you were
Confined within a field
Of probable causes

Decisions had been made
At a fast pace
Where making gains
Instead of losses
By finding buried treasures

Hidden near the surface
Of reality's turf
Were worth more
In sense rather than whole dollars
If you can take a hint

To *Live Like There's No Tomorrow*
On this playing field
Money has no value
In real time regarding
A well-known declining lifespan

Of *the borrower* or *the beholder*
For the sake of sanity's proportionate relevance
In terms of carrying out
Its plans for longevity's benefitting purposes
For the unknown

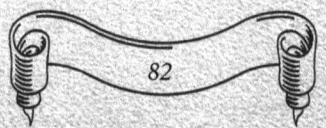

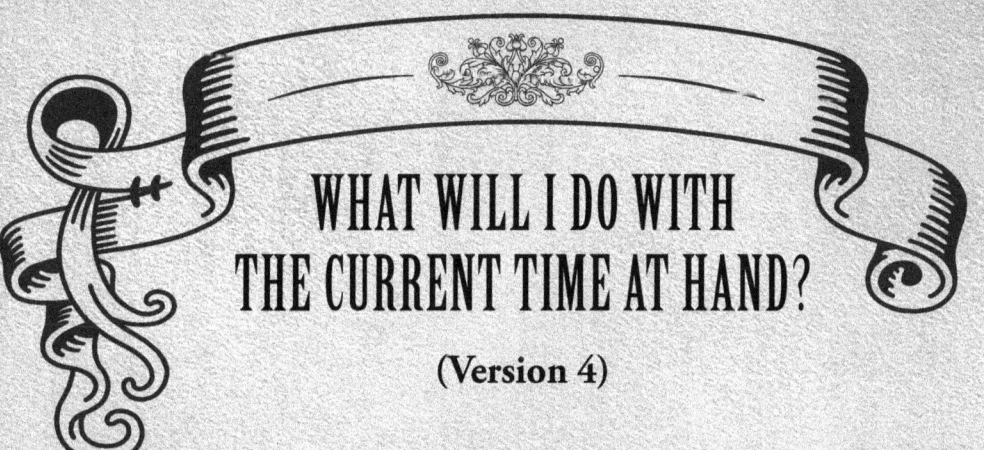

WHAT WILL I DO WITH
THE CURRENT TIME AT HAND?

(Version 4)

The sands within
This mystic hourglass
Have passed
Only to be
Stuck in the middle

Of random earthly destinies
Yet
I have to decide why
During *this evening* or *later tonight*
What shall I do with?

The remnants of my life
At this point in time
Alive and *Well*
From the start of this day
Each and *Every* step

Will prevail without delay
Taking command
For what lies before me
Promoting my evolution
Masterfully speaking my own language

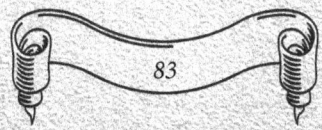

From the depths of my inhibitions
Forever allowed to comprehend
Reality's grip on my imagination
Unveiled to reveal a vague demand for
What Will I Do With The Current Time At Hand?

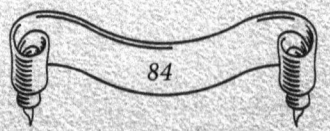

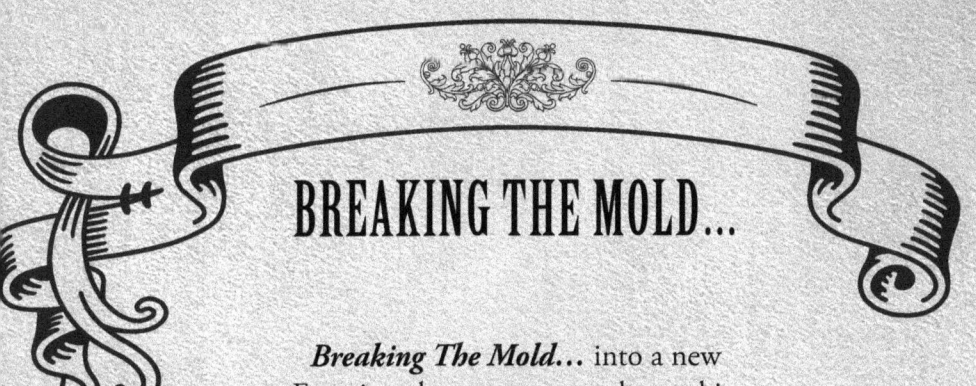

BREAKING THE MOLD...

Breaking The Mold... into a new
Frontier what was once sculptured in
The mind can further be chiseled
Into a new realty if beings can daringly admit
Within their own hearts that the truth

Beyond today's said uncertainty
Can and *Will* appear as long as
Participation acts have
Revered what perpetuates the *wealth* of a
New frontier's *consciousness*

www.ingramcontent.com/pod-product-compliance
Lightning Source LLC
Chambersburg PA
CBHW051548120626
46551CB00013B/1415